Experiential Learning: A Foundation for Social Work Education and Practice

Transforming Social Work:
Knowledge for the 21st Century

Council on Social Work Education Monograph Series

Experiential Learning: A Foundation for Social Work Education and Practice

Howard Goldstein

Council on Social Work Education
Alexandria, VA

Once again, to my beloved Linda
and to dear "Sadie"

Goldstein, Howard, 1922–
Experiential learning: a foundation for social work education and practice / Howard Goldstein.
p. cm. -- (Transforming social work)
Includes bibliographical references and index.
ISBN 0-87293-080-7
1. Social work education. I. Title. II. Series.
HV11.G66 2001
361.3'2'071073--dc21

00-011712

Manufactured in the United States of America

Contents

Foreword

Howard Goldstein's untimely death on November 1, 2000, prevented him from completing the final editing of this book. Because Howard had enlisted my assistance in reviewing the book and we shared similar approaches to practice and teaching, I was asked by his family and Michael Monti, director of publications and media for the Council on Social Work Education, to aid in this project. The work involved some clarification of content and the completion of some references.

My contributions to the content have been minor—Howard's writing speaks clearly for itself. As to the references, despite the efforts of the CSWE editorial staff, it has not been possible to complete all of them. Those familiar with his writing know that had Howard been able to complete the editing himself, the manuscript would have been fully referenced with his usual attention to detail and exactness.

Howard cared passionately about the ideas in this book. His last energies were spent on editing it with the help of his daughter, Jana Bouc. It gave him great satisfaction at the end of his life to know that it would be published. As a long time admirer of Howard, one who cherished his friendship and deeply respected his scholarship, it has been my privilege to participate in a small way in making this possible.

Ruth Grossman Dean, Professor
Simmons College School of Social Work

Preface

I was deeply honored by the invitation of the Council of Social Work Education Publications and Media Commission to submit a proposal for a book for their new series, Transforming Social Work: Knowledge for the 21st Century. The series is intended to challenge current professional thinking and offer fresh views about social work education. The topic assigned to me was field education.

As stated, the topic was certainly open-ended, restrained only by the requirement that it be challenging and offer fresh views. Yet these are scarcely restraints; they are, in fact, inducements to forsake the mainstream or the trail most often taken, and to cut new directions. As enticing as this offer is, it also bears the burden of responsibility. Like the pioneer concerned with new discoveries, the scholar concerned with fresh ideas and theories would be foolhardy to plunge ahead without proper preparation. As we will see in the pages that follow, it is important to be aware of the intellectual origins of the trail one is pursuing, the state of the art or nature of the immediate point of departure, whether others have already established some tentative pathways, and, of course, the goal that the new pathway might possibly achieve.

Field education always has been and continues to be an arena of professional education that is of critical concern to me. Forty years as a teacher of direct practice in four universities in both the United States and Canada at the master's and doctoral levels have involved me in every aspect of field education: establishing field placements, attempting to integrate class and field, training field instructors, and implementing studies of field practices, among others.

With the passing of years, my distress about the nature and direction of the experiential aspect of social work education has grown. Well-socialized to the standard model, I, like most educators, didn't give much thought to the possibility there might be an alternative to the separation of classroom and field. While not entirely seamless my own professional education did offer a sense of continuity between my classroom learning and my experience with practice in the field. I later came to appreciate that the reason for this consistency was that my education occurred in the pre-Ph.D. era. Both my classroom and field teachers were themselves seasoned practitioners, rich in experience, comfortable with the theoretical as well as the imaginative and intuitive talents that allow for the emergence of individual styles. Hierarchy was not an issue; both field and classroom teachers shared common principles about and expectations for how students should mature into capable social workers. There was an ongoing give-and-take between class and field. In the classroom we grappled with case material drawn from the field, which in turn enabled us to transfer this learning to work with real clients. Another integrating factor was the highly disciplined use of process recording that called on the student to capture and define the nature of the helping experience and his or her role and responsibility within it. Finally, learning was reinforced by that ever-dependable ritual called supervision; it was indeed the central component, the nexus of learning and time was regularly earmarked for this mentoring experience.

It is neither nostalgia nor the memory of an educational utopia that prompts me to resurrect these events. Rather, this account identifies a few fundamental principles of learning that are basic to a meaningful program of social work education. Irrespective of the content of the program, its theoretical orientation, its methodological approach, and so on, its integrity depends on (a) a strong measure of congruence between class and field, (b) the expectation that students will assume responsibility for their learning, and (c) field teachers who ensure the consistency, regularity, and dependability of the mentoring or supervisory process.

It has been difficult over the years to maintain these principles. Social agencies that offer opportunities for learning are under increasing pressures, including problems of funding, increasing demands for service, and a growing emphasis on managed care. The result of these pressures is that field education has lost many of its priorities. Field teachers, as I will show, are too frequently left to their own resources and often must resort to their own expeditious forms of teaching which may or may not conform to the school's program.

Despite the serious problems for educators and learners posed by the geographical, as well as the educational, separation of the academy and the field, the profession and its curricula continue to cling to the traditional "separatist" model of social work education. In this model the responsibility for "thinking" and knowledge development is assigned to the classroom and the responsibility for "doing" and skill development to the field. Numerous texts have been written in recent years to further strengthen and articulate the traditional model.

Reviewing the literature on field education, my experiences and observations as a field educator, and remembering the words of John Dewey and his followers, such as Donald Schön, I was persuaded that there was not much left to say about the concept of field education. Rather, the challenge, as it seemed to me, was to return to the universe of social work education and to ask how one learns to be a social worker. The answer to this question is that experience, or a shift from a teaching to a learning model, is the foundation for learning—not only in social work, as I will show, but in other professions as well. The development of this argument shapes the introductory section of this monograph.

The second section develops the social history and epistemology of social work education to explain how the profession arrived at its current scheme of preparation for professional practice. I consider, among other influences, the early shift from sentiment and philosophy to the scientific ideal. Here, as in other sections, the remarkable contributions of Jane Addams and John Dewey are examined. With the establishment of training schools the distinction between classroom and the field became solidified: the former became responsible for the transmission of a body of knowledge to students, the latter for providing the experience with which students begin to master practice skills.

This division has had its critics; the ideas of Bertha Reynolds, Charlotte Towle, and the Hollis-Taylor report are given careful notice. Beyond structure, the early content of social work education was strongly influenced by Mary Richmond. Over the years, various systems of thought rose and fell. They include psychoanalytic theory, the functional school of social work, and systems theory, to name a few. The emergence of the social sciences, and the proliferation of diverse methodologies and techniques like family therapy, reality therapy, and Gestalt therapy have also influenced content. This prelude to the explication of the Experiential Learning Model is summed up with a careful analysis of the flaws, limitations, and discontinuities that are consequences of the separation of class and field.

The section on learning and experience comprises the heart and purpose of this book. In this section I develop further the position that the field or practicum is the integral component of education for practice. An outline of the components and stages of learning introduces the balance of this section. The outline deals with the critical importance of students' talents (or, according to Howard Gardner, 1983, their multiple intelligences) and their unique learning styles. Also considered are the stages and contexts for learning with particular emphasis given to the importance of reflective learning, and critical discourse. Throughout, we look at the shifts that are required in the relation between classroom and field and between teacher and student when the experiential model supplants traditional models of learning.

The intent is to show the experiential learning model in action. After tracing its origins in medical education, examples of it applications in other fields (e.g., service learning in the liberal arts, student teaching in schools of education) I offer a vignette, a first-person account of how this learning was experienced over time. Although examples of this learning model in social work are sparse in the United States, well-developed programs in Britain and Australia offer persuasive examples.

Change in curriculum policy frequently arouses misgivings and resistance. Thus, the book concludes with an analysis of the obstacles that can confront the plan to implement a model of experiential learning. One among many is the question of how the role of the field teacher (or the "practice teacher" as he or she is known in Britain) might be enhanced.

Altogether, this book strives to present a coherent picture of an approach to professional education that best reflects current knowledge about how human beings learn. In many ways this approach matches our intuitive or common sense understanding of learning in everyday, in critical, and in purposive circumstances. As both survivors and achievers in a challenging world, we "know" that sometimes we muddle our way through challenges and at other times perform with unrealized proficiency. But one of the great challenges to learning is the need to "unlearn" the conventional wisdom that we have come to accept without question or reflection. It does not take too close a look to see that it is this challenge that makes social work practice so difficult. We are constantly asking our clients to rethink their lives, actions, and beliefs. As educators, can we ask less of ourselves?

Acknowledgment

With gratitude to the Publications and Media Commission of the Council of Social Work Education for their confidence in my ability to produce this book. I add special thanks to its past chair, Dean and Professor Ann Weick.

Part One

A Foundation for Social Work Education and Practice

One
Becoming a Social Worker: Teaching, Learning, and Reflection

How does one learn to become a social worker? At first glance, this may seem to be an artless question since social work education has become an established institution, a constituent of systems of higher education in the United States and in other countries throughout the world. Nearly a century has passed since the first training school for social workers opened in New York City, and at this writing 128 master's and more than 400 bachelor's programs have come into existence; 50 more are in candidacy status for accreditation by the Council on Social Work Education (CSWE). Such development could not occur without authoritative standards about education for professional practice.

As is true of any long-established institution—and particularly those of the academic variety—social work education is buttressed by countless documents designed to answer the question of how one learns to be a social worker. A national association, CSWE, was created to preserve and enhance the quality of social work education for practice. Social work programs accredited by CSWE outline their admissions and curricula in catalogs and other university publications. Curricula of these programs (also approved by CSWE) advise what should be taught programmatically. Course outlines and syllabi detail the specific content of courses and the educational objectives students are expected to achieve. Together, these documents provide the structure, content, and rationale that attempt to answer the question of how one learns to be a social worker.

Because social work is such a peculiar and, in some ways, extraordinary (and, some will add, still young) profession, we have to expect that as informative as such resources are, they are bound to fall short of settling the question. For one thing, emerging theories about the nature of human learning tend to keep the question alive. Educators not only need to be alert to these theories but also should be ready to reconsider their teaching philosophy and its effectiveness in light of them. Furthermore, questions about human learning need to be considered within the broad frame of the growing national concern about the effectiveness of higher education.

What do I mean by "the peculiar and extraordinary nature of social work" and what is its bearing on social work education? Consider the profession's optimistic and lofty mission and purpose as stated in CSWE's Curriculum Policy Statement (CPS). The CPS (1992) includes such objectives as the "alleviation of poverty, oppression, and discrimination"; attempting to help people to improve "personal well-being," "mental-health," or "social functioning"; and working for "family restoration," or "community development." These are fine topics for keynote speeches or shorthand commentaries in ordinary case records. But compared to the objectives of other professions, which are far more concrete and circumscribed, social work's goals look like ideals or abstractions. Taken together, these objectives seem extremely broad compared to what might be considered the objectives involved in the education of lawyers, doctors, and teachers. There is a considerable gap between the ideal and the real, between the archetype and the down-to-earth, experiential nature of everyday practice.

If we lower our sights a bit to glance at what it is that social workers actually need to know in relation to what they actually do, the question of how they learn becomes critical. This is because they must learn so much. Professional journals, which mirror the profession's endeavors, publish articles on issues as varied as adoption, disability, family violence, aging, poverty, and homelessness. These are just a sampling of the diverse problems that fall within the purview of social work. Even more ambitious and boundless is the universe of knowledge and practice that social workers are supposed to master. Like a set of Chinese nesting boxes, required knowledge about mind and body are encased within concepts of families and groups, which are in turn part of theories of community and society. On top of this are the many precepts that add the ideological flavor to the mastery of knowledge: social justice, human rights, and social welfare, for example. And to this array must be appended the generous collection of methods, techniques, interventions, and skills, the instruments of change that the learner must be able to select from and confidently put into practice. The array of knowledge required is so vast. How does a social work student find ways to approach it, digest it, and make it usable?

In my long and active career as both practitioner and educator I have wondered at the seemingly quixotic inspirations of so many social workers, their willingness to meet a daunting array of social problems head on and try to make a difference as they respond to the personal predicaments that await them every morning at their professional doorsteps. Surely, this spirit may be fundamental to good practice, but it is insufficient to assure effectiveness. We need to ask how learners, demonstrably willing to help, might be prepared to respond to the baffling rebuffs by the hostile client or the brittle family, or cope with clients whose values, culture, customs, and beliefs differ from their own. And given the noble mission of social work, we need to discover how learners begin to appreciate and contend with the deep-set social injustices, prejudices, and other inequities that engulf their clients. Can we say with some measure of clarity what students are really supposed to know and do to be effective, to make a meaningful difference in clients' lives?

Both literally and figuratively, these are something more than academic questions. They are experiential questions concerned with the instrumental and purposive character of professional practice. If nothing else, they urge us to think about where we might search for answers to the question of how students learn. Certainly many of the crises in practice mentioned above are incisively explored in the classroom. But they rise to the surface less rhetorically and with greater immediacy in the earthy, empirical context of the student's education—field instruction or the practicum, where learning contexts can be as diverse as a therapeutically focused mental health center, a neighborhood settlement, a school, or a community housing project.

Within such learning contexts the student confronts real life dilemmas, not in their molecular or abstract forms as defined by theories, models, or constructs but in their naturalistic and complex state. How does the student make the transition from the abstract to the real? I believe that it is the very immediate and real-life dilemmas that students experience in the field that help them organize their approach to learning. Thus, for this reason I argue that, in our search for answers, we need to turn to the field as the educational setting because it stimulates the process and sets the priorities on what, specifically, students need to learn. Reversing the traditional arrangement, we can then consider how the classroom can support the field with knowledge that is directly relevant to practice with people. It is in the field that learners can gain the confidence, the talent, the art, and the proficiencies necessary to become competent social workers not only in their encounters with clients, but also with agencies, communities, and other constituents of real-life practice.

To put this another way, the practicum is the linchpin of social work education, where theory and practice might be linked, where some measure of integration can take place. The classroom offers instruction in the theoretical knowledge, the ideology, and the various intellectual systems that shape the firm foundations of practice. The field represents the verifiable and dynamic world of practice. Again, this world includes not only clients and their complex and often ambiguous problems, but also their families, the community, and the social agency itself, each abounding with competing and often contradictory rules and norms, political and economic pressures, and other expectations that complicate the basic act of helping. Certainly class and field are not as dichotomous I make them—if only for the sake of argument. Still, the field is the setting where the student painfully discovers, for example, that discrimination, prejudice, hate, and other noxious conditions are more than concepts and may be part of the agendas of social sectors which are not at all sanguine about the well-being of those in difficulty. It is in this snarl of complex and competing energies where learning becomes critical, where the need for special knowledge and skills becomes evident, where personal and professional values are put to the test. It is also the stage on which the novice can begin to discover his or her special talents and intuitions that might encourage, as social work literature puts it, a creative and inventive "use of self." The field is where knowledge, skill, personal and professional values, and creative talents are harmonized within the flow and process of experiential learning.

This book will demonstrate that experiential learning and its major context, the practicum, are the integral components of the whole of education for professional practice. Experiential learning is a humanistic and democratic model of education that prepares learners to respect, respond to, and find meaning in the impelling life experiences of their clients—the situational, cultural, spiritual, aesthetic, linguistic, and moral as well as the psychological and social. This approach to learning is fundamentally rooted in the educational philosophy of John Dewey. In his view, experience is the catalyst that links theory and practice. Dewey's philosophy is democratic insofar as it emphasizes the importance of human rights and needs within relationships, the community, and society (Dewey, 1916, 1925, 1938).

This broad and inclusive lens enlarges our appreciation of the extraordinary tasks that social workers face every day. Certainly the social and behavioral sciences allow for the most *objective* grasp and explanation of the many conditions that crowd into and shape the human experience. But reliance on such knowledge alone may lead us to overlook a complementary realm of wisdom that can enlighten us about the *subjective* meanings of that experience. A humanistic model of education should be receptive to the insights of the arts and humanities, fields that have engaged and explored the often baffling questions about the human condition. The humanistic approach to learning places value on examining the particular enigmatic, ironic, paradoxical, moral, heroic, tragic, and comic qualities of life that color the way we make our way in the world.

The adoption of a humanistic model of education, as I will show, signifies a shift from a teaching model to a learning model of education. In general terms, a teaching model is didactic, deductive, "top-down." In contrast, a learning model is experiential, inductive, and "bottom-up." An example of the teaching model is the conventional classroom setting where knowledge is aimed at achieving certain required objectives and imparted in an organized, sequential, and controlled style. The learning model involves a process of a different order. It is an experience that involves one's total self—mind and body, intellect and emotion, memory and foresight. It is an active and interactive process: one experiences and engages in learning. In the learning model learning is not necessarily sequential or linear; it can occur tangentially, by association, as one idea, now or later, triggers other insights, spinning in many directions at once. Learning that is more than rote and immediately practical is sometimes ironic. This is often the case in social work where students acquire objective knowledge and practical skills that are often peripheral and at times irrelevant to the fluid, sometimes messy, and subjective nature of the client's story and circumstances.

Clarification of the two models of education points to a specific recommendation. Although we need to attend to the enduring question of what students should be taught in social work education, this endeavor needs to take into account the questions of how, when, and under what circumstances people learn. More specifically, we need to ask how adults learn, especially those entering a profession concerned with the complexities of human relations. Education that takes into account the learning process within the context of adult development insures that learning constitutes a more comprehensive function in one's life than "a mere transmission of knowledge" from teacher to student (Montessori, 1967).

The opportunities for experiential learning provided by field instruction or other forms of active learning complement a humanistic approach to education. In the pages that follow I will develop this argument, showing how the various forms of this approach to learning are important not only to professional social work education, but also to the ongoing growth and development of the student and practitioner. It is important, first, to reflect on some questions on the teaching and learning involved in preparing a student to be a social worker. And before any revisions in the current educational paradigm can be contemplated, it is essential that we take a look at its origins, underlying assumptions, and current dilemmas. With this discussion as a background, it will then be possible to frame certain emerging ideas about intelligence, learning, and motivation that form the supports for experiential learning and a redesign of the relationship between the classroom and the practicum.

Teaching, Learning, and Reflection

"What to teach?" If memory serves, I believe this was a question posed by Helen Harris Perlman many years ago in one of her fine essays on social work education. It was a timely question some 30 years ago when I was preparing to teach my first social casework class to master's students. Little did I know that even now, almost 10 years since I taught my last direct practice class, this question would still be urgent and elusive.

The question about what to teach in those anxious moments 30 years ago was far more practical than philosophical. Given the plethora of advertisements and flyers that now clutter the educator's desk heralding this or that latest textbook on practice, it may be hard to imagine that back then there were comparatively few readings to assign. Professional journals were equally few in number. Finally, there was not the profusion of theories, now so available, from which the teacher could pick and choose to fill lectures and encourage discussion. As a freshly minted teacher I knew I was lightly armed with only my 10 years of professional experience and whatever intellectual matter I could salvage from my inconsiderable doctoral education. Then, as now, doctoral studies offered no preparation (except for certain role models) for answering the important question of how to teach—that is, the principles and theories of education that relate to the transmission of knowledge and the enhancement of learning processes. Social work education has operated under the illusory assumption that one only needs to be armed with specialized content in order to prepare students for professional practice, a state of affairs I will examine more closely in the last section of this work.

As I was focused only on what to teach, I wondered if perhaps I could find something worth teaching in my collection of notes and other fugitive pieces from my master's education. I skipped quickly through my human behavior loose-leaf, crammed with its hard-core psychoanalytic schemes and the dense scribbled pages of social welfare notes, before I found my casework notebook. Except for doodles and cryptic references to assignments long forgotten, there was nothing to show in my notebook for two years of class work.

Since that was the case, I had to ask myself, *how did we learn?* After all, my fellow students and I did manage to meet credentialing requirements and went on to assume professional roles and positions of responsibility. The stuff that crammed my other notebooks, the notes I dutifully recorded in every class, recalled traces of facts and knowledge. But astonishingly, of the single course that inspired my education and career, John Milner's casework class, there was no trace, no visible record. There was nothing but blank pages absent of the kind of articulate wisdom that I hoped would enable me to impart something intelligible to my social work students. The evidence that my fellow students and I learned a great deal in Mr. Milner's class wasn't on the page, and the answer to how we learned won't be found either in a grand educational design or in explicit educational objectives. Nonetheless, there was something implicitly meaty and natural in our learning process. Retrospectively I can give this process a name; we learned "experientially." We didn't learn this way by design or plan because "experiential learning" or its current analogue, "active learning," was not fashionable in those times—certainly not in social work education.

Mr. Milner's classroom looked like the others in which we acquired knowledge about human behavior, research, and social welfare. But he was not like most of our other teachers who lectured, gave written assignments, and evaluated our scholarship. John Milner and his kind were *mentors*: it was not so much *what* he taught as *how* he taught. It was not what we learned that counted; it was how we grew as emerging professional social workers. Mr. Milner, like most casework instructors in those years, did not have a doctoral education. His strong suit was direct practice. His summers and other free time were given to practice in different agencies to stay in professional form and keep pace with changes occurring in the field. He was fluent in theories of behavior and change (Mr. Milner was a Freudian). But with one teacherly foot in the field of practice, this abstract knowledge was always graphic and alive. When he spoke of such concepts as "defense mechanisms," "confrontation," or "countertransference," he used them not as cold abstractions but in the way a good storyteller fashions an interesting tale. Such terms became less pretentious and even reassuring when he would let us know we were not alone in struggling with our self-doubts. He, for example, confessed to his own frustration (countertransference?) in trying to get a closed up, withdrawn kid (defense mechanism?) to realize just how angry he was (confrontation?). The formality of these imposing concepts thawed in the warming light of human experience. Gradually Mr. Milner's version of social work practice, informed by my own experience and thinking, became my own.

The steady focus of this class on the real-life nature of practice meant that the division between class and field was more geographical than real. "Integration of theory and practice" (only a budding ideal at that time) was achieved more by circumstance than by plan. Much of the class content was comprised of the cases students were struggling with in the field, cases that were fresh, perplexing, and, for all concerned, very urgent. Insights gained in the class were, in turn, tried out in the field, with the expectation that "how it worked" would subsequently be reported back to the class. My recollections, certainly romanticized by the passing of time, suggest at best a kind of Socratic utopia where dialogue and discourse leads to the truth; more likely, what occurred was intellectual floundering or hit-or-miss attempts to make sense of what seemed like pure chaos. Speculations lurched from one extreme to another as we tried to understand not only a particular client's predicament but, more often, as fumbling novices, our own. Of course we were not bereft of intellectual tools. Mr. Milner's brand of scholarship, the readings he assigned, and other theoretical content gave both structure and substance to the experiential nature of learning but mostly by accident or coincidence. Because cases from the field filled so much of our class time, frequently theory and practice glanced off one another, resulting in some minor epiphanies of the "Aha!" or "Now I see!" order. Such providential moments perhaps explain the barrenness of my notebook: the notes or information that we imprint on the page scarcely compare in power with the knowledge gained from experience that is imprinted in neural networks of the brain.

There was yet another mode of learning and knowing: process recording. Like any eager learners, we would have welcomed prescriptions for practice, recipes for what to do, when, and with whom. It would have been much easier if we, like journeyman carpenters or plumbers, could have collected the proper tools and proceeded to fix that which needed fixing. Process recording was the antidote to the craving for such quick fixes. The regular assignment to reflect on the client interview and untangle its process, attempting to explain and interpret the nuances of the relationships and the twists and turns over time, was a tough one. If this attempt to create order and meaning was not challenging enough, there was the potential humiliation involved in having to submit this personally charged document to one's instructor for careful dissection and critique. It is easier to praise this exercise in retrospect, for process recording often drained the spirit and awakened self-doubt. Still, there is little that compares to the creative but uncanny moment when, inexplicably, the ragged edges of theory and practice, of knowing and doing, click together like the last piece of a baffling puzzle. A full mind serves one better than a brimming notebook. Call it integration.

Or call it "reflective thinking" or "reflective judgment." The maturation of reflective thinking depends on a learning climate that knowingly promotes hypothetical speculation, but it can also result from uninvited bewilderment and confusion. For example as a student, I found it necessary to juggle two contradictory theories of human behavior and change while trying to adapt to two conflicting roles—a student subject to the evaluation of my teachers, and a rookie professional trying to be "effective" with my clients. As I mentioned, my casework teacher was firmly identified with the Diagnostic school (Freudian-deterministic). But my field instructor was a member of the Functionalist school, whose perspectives on theory and practice were distinctly contrary to those of the Diagnostic school. To put it simply, Freudians stress the importance of unconscious and deterministic influences of childhood experiences whereas Functionalists (or followers of Otto Rank) discredit this idea, insisting that the here and now counts most. In the case of my client, Mrs. Potts, who couldn't manage her obstinate son, my Diagnostic casework teacher advised me to inquire into this mother's early relationship with her father since that might illuminate her deep-seated confusion about authority and control. My Functionalist field instructor, in contrast, thought that it would be helpful to strengthen my relationship with Mrs. Potts, to help her use my support for discovering greater confidence in her parental role. Who was right?

Faced with such powerful contrarieties, it must have been the obligation I felt to my client and her pressing situation that caused me to turn inward and ponder how I might make sense of the dilemma. Much later, Schön (1983) identified this mental strategy as "reflective thinking," thought patterns that are activated when habitual routines of problem solving don't work or when the usual theoretical prescriptions are no longer dependable. It takes considerable time and testing before one can trust, even enjoy, this imaginative side of the mind. Without these constraints and with growing confidence I gradually learned that, for example, from their perspectives or ideologies both my instructors could be right in how they perceived the human situation. A journey with Mrs. Potts into her memory and reconstruction of her first decade of life would tell me something about her "truths." But they would indeed be *her* truths, selectively sorted and arranged into a story that, for her, might explain or make a bit of sense out of her present predicament. Looking at the here and now of Mrs. Potts's circumstances would disclose more immediate concerns. As a reflective practitioner it was my job to sift through competing perspectives to construct an effective approach to working with Mrs. Potts.

Perspectives on life are neither final nor mutually exclusive, and empirical truths about the human situation, especially about behavior and change—*the* complete theory, *the* effective method—are not "out there" waiting to be discovered, learned, and applied in a standard mode. Acquired knowledge is fragile and provisional, ever ready to be supplanted by progress in genetics, neurophysiology, developmental biology, contextual studies, and other disciplines that discredit artificial separations of brain, mind, body, and place. And this "hard" knowledge is complemented by the "softer" knowledge of what it means to be human. Any encounter in practice inevitably must take account of such issues as gender, social justice, personal and shared rights, ethical and moral choices and obligations, and belief systems. The contingency of knowledge makes learning much more complex and challenging than if we could simply arm ourselves with the universal truth or the effective method. In the absence of such absolutes, reflective judgement is imperative for navigating one's way through both personal and professional problem solving. And in many ways coming to terms with the idea that knowledge is not unitary, that it can take many forms and that understanding is never complete, can loosen the learner and practitioner from the illusory obligation to be the expert. Many pathways to understanding appear when one feels the freedom to join with a client in a mutual search for more rewarding ways of living in the world.

Logic and good judgment prescribe that knowledge about how people learn should inform what should be taught. But like all seemingly obvious equations, the product is not that easy to achieve. Implicitly, the two questions seem to be interdependent: the question of how people learn depends on assumptions about what they should be learning and vice versa. Explicitly, this doesn't seem to be the case. Social work curriculum builders and instructors talk about what they think students ought to know. The Council on Social Work Education Curriculum Policy Statement that guides any program's curriculum is replete with categories of educational content, delineated in varying degrees of precision. These categories are, it is good to note, often accompanied by precisely stated objectives: demonstrable evidence of what the student should learn. But little is added about how this learning is supposed to occur. While class and field are commonly considered different learning experiences, questions like whether one should study ethical issues in practice the same way one learns about developmental stages, or family structure, or the history of social welfare issues never seem to arise. Apparently, social work educators' assumptions about *how* students will learn what is taught is an unquestioned given. My intent is to question this given.

How does one learn? A perennial question that invites definitions both pompous and profound, that evokes the visions of great thinkers from Aristotle ("To learn is a natural pleasure, not confined to philosophers, but common to all people") to Shakespeare ("Learning is but an adjunct to our self. And where we are our learning likewise is") to Hegel ("Education is the act of making man ethical"). The standard dictionary compounds the definition by referring to gaining knowledge or mastery through study or experience, memorizing, acquiring an ability or skill, awareness, discovering, and more. Fundamentally, learning is what we do—at times, from moment to moment—to preserve our worth and to stay safe, secure, and alive.

But these definitions become less Platonic, not so lofty, when we narrow the inquiry to how one learns to become a responsible, ethical professional who, not necessarily by invitation, enters into the life circumstances of other human beings with the intent of achieving some form of change. Taking the next step by inquiring what this nebulous word change implies, we find ourselves muddling around in rather swampy terrain. For change can mean whatever the speaker or practitioner decides it means, whether it involves one's psyche, behavior, existence, or ecology. Achieving change can take the form of attempting to cure or alleviate symptoms of morbidity and psychopathology, or it can take the form of searching for the client's strengths to enhance and support resiliency. The goals of change may be as diverse as empowerment, improved social adjustment, social control, or social functioning, better problem solving, heightened self-esteem, hopefulness, and spiritual gratification. And even more confusing, these goals may be multiple or overlapping.

The question of how one learns is answered conveniently by the empirical minded with the edict "science does provide a solution" (Thyer & Myers, 1998). In this view, one learns to base one's practice solely on research, studies of methods and techniques of treatment that purport to produce effective outcomes. This is a tempting but facile solution that begs the question of what "effective" means. We are back again to the original definition—effective means whatever the practitioner, the expert and guiding force, decides it means—which results in an exercise in tautology. To be sure, the "ethical" social worker may propose a "contract" with his client to establish mutuality and partnership. However, since assessment, diagnosis, treatment plan, and preferred outcomes (major topics in most social work practice textbooks) are framed within the practitioner's system of practice and professional lexicon, clients have little choice but to comply if they want help. Moreover, all parties must accept the unstated assumption that it is indeed ethical for one human being (properly credentialed) to determine the changes and goals that are appropriate for other people.

A humanistic-educational perspective offers a more liberal answer to the question of how learning is achieved. The helping experience becomes truly mutual, a partnership, when clients are regarded as experts about their lives and thus have something to say about the goals of helping that are "right" for them. This is, in fact, the essential step toward the greater goal of taking responsibility for one's life. Optimally, "how things should be" should be defined by their parlance, in terms that are therefore meaningful to them. To be sure, while the client's version might not be as analytic and profound as the practitioner's, it would be more pertinent, however, to his or her life's circumstances.

I will deal with the question of how one learns to be a responsible and ethical social worker within the ethos of a humanistic-educational frame of reference in the balance of this work. But as an end point for this introduction and a starting point for what follows I want to sum up the assumptions about meaningful and rich learning that are coincident with humanistic learning. For humanistic learning aims for more than just practicality and efficiency, more than the acquisition of knowledge and refinement of skill. All are, of course, essential but not entirely sufficient, since we deal with lives in flux, not objects in space subject to control.

❋ ❋ ❋

The slice of autobiography and commentary that introduced this book yields a set of principles, markers for later reference, to support the argument for humanistic learning in the field of experience.

- Learning is a narrative process that is active and experiential. It is dialogical (or more accurately, triadic, considering the role of culture in human relations) rather than linear or unidirectional.

- Learning occurs in many ways, sometimes idiosyncratically, not always subject to categories. It may be deductive when grounded knowledge is imparted or acquired, inductive when knowledge is developed from experiential observation and participation, or vicarious as when one learns empathetically through the perceived or narrated experiences of others.

- The proper form of teaching in a humanistic sense is mentoring, a collegial and Socratic approach.

- Reflective thinking is the attribute of the true learner. It is an approach to reality that is both confident and open-ended. It is confident in the sense that what one knows is for the time accepted as authentic though not absolute. It is open-ended in the sense that one is amenable to new or contradictory evidence.

Few would disagree that the reflective (and one may add, the analytical) thinker is the ideal product of education. Certainly this learner is the product of the kind of education that encourages a trace of humility and imagination in the face of the trials and enigmas of human circumstances. I find the metaphor "liberal ironist" a more inspiring and lively allusion to such a thinker, for the reflective thinker is not a contemplative philosopher but an active inquirer who marvels at her world and who is driven by curiosity and questioning. It is a term coined by Richard Rorty (1989), the modern American pragmatist philosopher. Rorty's work builds on the themes of earlier pragmatists, William James and John Dewey, who viewed knowledge as *activity* rather than contemplation (Kolenda, 1990). To put it another way, in the view of these pragmatists knowledge is *functional*. Whether it is based on perception, observation, concepts, or theories, knowledge serves the ongoing process of successful adaptation to the contingencies and demands of experience. Thus, the incentive for learning is enlivened not only by concern, but also by the hope and possibility for finding better, more rewarding ways of coping with experience. Modern pragmatists' view that knowledge is not absolute or final parallels ideas about knowing and understanding that have in recent years been flowing into mainstream social work thought. These include social constructionism, the awareness of how language is shaped by culture and society; hermeneutics, the study of meaning in language and communication; and phenomenology and existential thought.

How does the pragmatists' conception of knowledge translate into the education of the "liberal ironist," particularly as it pertains to social work? First, let us define "liberal" and "ironist." To begin with, forget the invective that has been heaped on liberalism in recent years and consider the term "liberal" in its small "l," nonpolitical or nonideological sense. As it is generally understood, a liberal is one who values a truly democratic way of life, who is actively committed to social justice and the general good. But as "we-conscious" as the liberal may be, she is also striving to redefine and reinvent herself. In its humanistic and active sense, liberalism connotes an openness to others' outlooks and beliefs, a willingness not only to understand but also to make sure that one's own perspective does not obscure the other's right to an outlook. I found a useful example of this kind of liberalism in a eulogy to Supreme Court Justice, William Powell (in Westin, 1998):

> Though the consummate judge, Powell dealt with people as they were, not just as clients or employees or adversaries. He listened to all sides: he understood the theoretical as well as the practical; he knew that sometimes how someone reached a decision was as important as the decision itself. He had the courage to face facts as they were, not as he would like them to be. And in that Justice Powell represented the best we could hope to become: a genuinely wise man for whom balanced judgment represented a prime virtue. (p. 29)

Powell, in other words, was committed to a kind of openness that allowed one to see the limits of one's own position without giving it up. One could hold onto one's values and, at the same time, entertain contradictory views.

In its metaphorical sense, we might consider the "ironist" as one who has learned to live comfortably with uncertainty, ambiguity, and the absence of final explanations. The perfect irony in Socratic terms is the acknowledgment, "I know that I do not know." This does not mean that the ironist is a nihilist who has forsaken the possibility of knowing the world and its people. Rather, like the reflective practitioner we will be considering, the ironist is boldly and energetically alert to other possibilities, other meanings, and other subtleties that make up even the ordinary human experience. He or she is, in a manner of speaking, like the Talmudist (and, as some wit added, the neurotic) who can see both sides of the question at the same time.

While the ironist is not averse to the facts and knowledge that a good, sober textbook or theorist can offer, he knows that what he garners from such sources is a tentative approximation of reality, one footprint among others in the pathway of knowledge. He isn't bound by a special ideology, but at the same time he can appreciate that useful values and "truths" may be revealed even in the most extreme dogmas. In the final analysis, the ironist is most at home with and draws his strength from literature—the novels, dramas, and poetry that portray the paradox, dark humor, and incongruities of the human dilemma.

In social work practice perhaps the best example of the liberal ironist, or reflective thinker, is the imaginative family therapist who is less interested in reducing the curious characters of a family to a structure or diagnosis than in attempting to unravel and help rewrite the family's drama or story. For a family, almost by definition, is shot through with irony in action. Irony reigns in the gaps between what people say and what they mean, between how their words are intended and how they are interpreted, between what people deserve and what they get. Twists of fate and the workings of the culture and society in which the family strives to survive can also be ironic. Irony is central in the stories the family tells about itself. Indeed, this irony is celebrated in the diaries, essays, autobiographies, novels, and plays that comprise great literature.

The Social Worker as Reflective Practitioner

Thus far, I have spoken in general, and perhaps idealistic, terms about the outlook on the human drama and about kinds of thinking that need to be developed for entry into the lives and circumstances of other human beings. But it is important to frame a more specific answer to the question of how one learns to be a social worker within the pragmatics of teaching and learning. The most direct answer, as I have indicated, is that one learns to be a social worker experientially and actively. The prescription for developing the talents, imagination, and style necessary for helping as a practicing social worker is not far different from the advice offered to those who aspire to develop their special creative abilities. It has been said, for example, if you want to be a writer, then write. If you want to be a practicing social worker, then practice.

The aspiring writer will, for starters, run head on into questions about audience, style, voice, medium, and plot, among other issues. Likewise, the aspiring social worker will come face-to-face (literally and figuratively) with quandaries on meeting the stranger called the "client." "Preparation for practice" is a comforting platitude used by educators. It implies that consternation will be reduced if the learner gets enough rehearsal time in the safe, abstract, and theoretical harbor of the classroom. That premise deserves closer scrutiny since it promises that the problem will be relieved when, in fact, it is only delayed. Every human encounter proves to be, in important ways, like no other. Each interview is a new ball game.

But what is the assumption about learning underlying the idea that time in the classroom will prepare students for practice in the field? Sheafor and Jenkins (1982) are among the few scholars in social work education who even consider this question. They assert quite logically that "once assumptions are made about student learning, the social work program must develop objectives for each curriculum area" (p. 9). However, the authors seem to settle for just one learning scenario, the familiar "knowing-understanding-doing" paradigm. In this view learning involves the acquisition and storing of knowledge (knowing) that becomes intelligible in relation to explaining specific situations (understanding), and is then applied to real-life events (doing). Nonetheless, the authors acknowledge that this formula for learning will not answer other questions about field instruction. The authors ask, for example, whether field instruction should be an integral part of the curriculum where clearly specified content is taught or the culminating experience where the student applies the classroom content.

The knowing-understanding-doing paradigm offers a rather cramped version of human learning as a linear, input-output task, a means to an end. It is indeed a useful method when practical problem-solving is all that is required. For example, on setting up my new fax machine, I acquire new information from the manual, and try to memorize the procedures that I hope will work when I try to apply them to sending a message. But this banking metaphor for learning has limited applications for the kinds of complex, emotion-laden, and ironic problems of living that ordinarily challenge social workers. More importantly, this learning paradigm is just one of a series of schemes that have bolstered the traditional separation between class and field.

Any assumption about how people learn must take account of the actual process of learning and the principles of learning that support the process. The idea of learning as a process will lead us into a closer study of the phenomenology of the learning event: what is occurring, who is involved, and for what ends? I will consider the principles of learning, the ideologies and events that led to current conventions of teaching and learning in social work, in the next chapter.

Dimensions of the Learning Process

To put it simply, learning is a process involving a particular environment and a particular purpose. There are four synchronous and interrelated dimensions of learning: the learner, the learning content, the learning context, and the purpose of learning (see Goldstein, 1981b). In the paragraphs that follow, I will discuss each dimension in general terms, except for the section on learning content where I deal with the particularities of social work content.

The Learner. The learner is not a yearling passively waiting to be filled and fattened with knowledge, but the active and intentional agent of the learning process. The dispositions, attitudes, talents, styles, and other characteristics of the learner inevitably determine the meaning of the learning experience in both nuanced and explicit ways. The learner is the true embodiment of *meaning* in its richest sense. The growth and maturation of the learner, or for that matter her or his grasp of a new insight that was not apparent before, is a celebratory, meaningful event. Equally, learning will open new vistas of knowledge and experience yet to be known. The teacher is a valued collaborator in the learning event, and the fruits of learning will have meaning for others encountered by the learner.

Content. Content is the substance we want the student to master. Looking at the curricula of social work programs of the past, or even glancing at the diversity of curricula in current social work programs, tells us that the question of what students should know to become proficient social workers is an enduring one. And the question is further clouded by uncertainty about the definition of "proficient." The vagaries of history themselves ensure that knowledge and methods that are relevant for one era become moot in the next. For example, the fresh knowledge in the social sciences about social systems was instrumental in the shift from teaching methods of practice (social casework, social group work, and community organization) to a generalist model. The changing tides of society's needs and the specific needs of the diverse constituencies served by the profession also find their way into the changing curriculum. Just a glance at any professional journal will show that social workers are gathering their resources to work with old and young, minorities and cultures, disabilities, families of every variety, and the array of social problems that reflect the state of modern society.

The ambitious effort to keep up to date with social change is not helped by the many questions that bear on the selection of knowledge that is appropriate for educational purposes. It is not just a matter of what should be selected but a more fundamental issue of what actually constitutes knowledge. At one extreme, positivists lay claim to what they assume are empirical and verifiable "truths"; at the other extreme, we find the postmodernists who are far less optimistic about the possibility of certain and final answers. Social work educators wend their ways between the two extremes, interrupted by occasional and sometimes fierce bouts of polemics. The result is that, among the curricula (and even within the same curriculum) of graduate and undergraduate programs, knowledge content is often selective or arbitrary.

There is yet another way of looking at this puzzle. Although all graduates earn the same credentials, they are not equally equipped, if that is the right term, with the same knowledge of and approaches to the human problems they will eventually encounter. Again, almost by the luck of the draw, a student's orientation to methods of inquiry, methodology, problem definition, philosophy of change, and so on are likely to be influenced by any of a number of contingencies. These include the courses she happens to fall into, the professor's particular point of view, and the quality of field placements and the opportunities for learning they provide. Perhaps the question of what should constitute the ideal curriculum cannot be finally answered. Perhaps this is all to the good: only vigorous and provocative debate and critical discourse will ensure the vitality and resonance of our social profession.

Context. Inseparable from the preceding dimensions of the process of learning, the dimension of context reminds us that learning does not occur in a physical or social vacuum. This process always takes place in some particular setting, within a particular social or institutional climate and its expectations, and at a certain time. The specific context imposes its own demands on both teachers and students. Obviously the nature of teaching and learning will be shaped by such structural conditions as the allocation of time—whether, for instance, the teaching module fills a semester, a quarter, or an accelerated program. Even the time of day counts, as teachers know. Early morning or late day classes, for example, pose their own problems with regard to the readiness to learn. And the physical environment and its climate make a difference, an issue that will earn further study when we consider the balance between and separation of class and field.

Purpose. In many ways, purpose is a baffling concept when it applies to education. However, learning that has no purpose, learning that is digested without appetite, is pointless, lost labor. Purpose may be explicit, as when we set objectives for a course or curriculum, stating directly what we intend to achieve. Or it may be implicit, as when we say that certain knowledge is good for its own sake. But purpose is not easily contained. It can express an immediate need (how to get from here to there, or what do I need to know to pass a test), it can be adaptive (what do I need to know to be comfortable in a new community), or purpose might signify a long-range vision and hope. And since purpose is an inner energy, a mixture of personal intentions and aims that are not always articulated, there is plenty of room for tension and troubling cross-purposes in the process of learning.

The classroom provides ample opportunities for such cross-purposes. I am sure that serious teachers must pause frequently, wondering what students really had in mind during a lecture or discussion. When I was teaching, the habits of my group work experience prompted me to scan the faces and postures of my students. Fastened to their classroom chairs, some were busily taking notes, others were giving me what looked like rapt attention; more than a few however, seemed inert, inscrutable. Were there any hints that might tell me whether, literally and figuratively, we were on the same page?

In my practice class, active role plays in which students enacted clinical encounters sometimes relieved some of my questioning, for there, in the improvisational theater we created, were performances revealing learning (and often talents) that students had actually acquired. My visits to their field placements were even more illuminating. Often, at the placement, I discovered there was little correspondence between the compliant student I thought I knew in my classroom and the audacious novice in her agency setting. The contrast between someone reading for a role in an audition and another stepping with purpose and measured confidence onto the live stage came to mind.

Essential Purposes of the Learning Process

The alert and caring teacher will strive to assure that the purposes of the educational program, the immediate learning experience, and the students' own purposes are not too far out of alignment. However, there is a set of generic purposes that should govern the process of educational preparation for professional practice. This set includes *socialization, knowledge building,* and *growth enhancement,* the foundations on which the progression of "becoming" a professional rest. Although these purposes are the sine qua non of professional education, they cannot be defined with precision, achieved in universal terms, or in accord with explicit standards. Perhaps, under the rubric of knowledge building, we can say something in general terms about what one ought to know. But *if* socialization and growth are achieved, *how* they are achieved is another question.

Socialization. How one becomes socialized and how one matures depend on the character and virtues one brings to learning in the first place. And how they inform and guide the professional are inseparable from how he or she generally goes about the business of being a social worker. For the term socialization should not suggest that students are stamped out in identical forms, that knowledge is acquired in the same way, or that maturation occurs in a programmed fashion. Becoming a personal and professional self is the result of a seamless blend of these educational purposes.

Socialization begins to take hold when novices are inspired to identify with and become part of the mission, ethos, and culture of the profession. Such inspiration, as I have already suggested, might have been the compelling force for the selection of social work as a career. Saleebey (1999), in his eloquent personal essay on his own emergence as a social worker, mentor, and scholar, speaks of his "intellectual and axial devotion and passions and what it was about them that fired my ardor in the first place." He goes on to suggest that finding his calling in social work resulted in part from the sense of identification he felt with teachers who served as role models and with the heritage of social work symbolized in the works of Mary Richmond, Bertha Reynolds, and others. He reports also the excitement of "reading and hearing certain ideas."

Socialization is much more than just an intellectual knowledge of the profession's values, norms, and ethics. It implies a certain identity with all that is noble and progressive in the profession's existence, as well as a commitment to recognizing its failings and fighting for renewal of its integrity. In whatever ways the experience of socialization unfolds, it is rarely free of strain and ambivalence. By definition socialization means learning and acquiring certain values and standards that will necessitate relinquishing other beliefs and biases, perhaps with some personal discomfort and doubt. Socialization further implies the readiness to engage in dissent, and to be on the alert for threats to the ideals and integrity of one's vocation.

Knowledge Building. Compared to socialization, building knowledge appears to be a purpose one can define in concrete terms. Still, as Bertha Reynolds (1942) surmised many years ago, "learning an art, which is knowledge applied to doing something in which the whole person participates, cannot be carried on solely as an intellectual process, no matter how clearly and attractively subject matter is presented" (p. 69).

Growth Enhancement. Entwined with the first two, the educational aim of growth enhancement is the most critical of the three learning purposes and, at the same time, perhaps the most enigmatic. While growth should be a deliberate and conscious aim of professional education, it is at the same time a natural, evolving process that should accrue (unless the practitioner is blinded by technique and theory) in ways that constantly enrich the character, style, and potential of the social worker. The ability to find meaning and reason in others' lives in the endeavor to be of service is important. But in the same beat, one discovers that such understanding is always tentative, that each probable answer only incites more perplexing questions. Can one arrive at a final answer about the ironies of aging and dying, the masked struggles of adolescence, or the unforeseen crises of parenthood? For learners to grow both personally and professionally, they needed to be prepared to give up on old answers and take on new ones. They need to stand ready, in the face of death or birth, crisis or trauma, suffering or joy, to give up former beliefs and certainties and take on all that can be learned from each novel experience.

Learning to be a social worker must be seen as more than a receptive process or a computational form of information processing in which students attempt to ingest information delivered from the outside by lectures and books for later retrieval. Perhaps only in tacit terms, the Functionalist school recognized the challenges that go with learning in one of its maxims: there is no growth without pain. As a teacher I came to understand that learning involved tension and distress, at least for my serious students. There were always students who passed through the educational experience with their shopping cart, picking off and taking with them the information and skills needed to be credentialed as a professional. But others were more earnest learners who painfully coped with the realization that becoming a social worker was not a terminal process. The learning they gained only revealed their remaining ignorance.

The best that serious learners can hope for are some resting points where they might develop the confidence they need for the demands of their ongoing journey. They have to gradually come to terms with the realization that the most enticing theories and methods are promissory but not predictive, that clients will (for good reasons) stubbornly frustrate their well-meaning desire to help. They will also find that the most estimable of the profession's values are often ignored, if not defeated, by the self-interests of bureaucracies. Perhaps most grievous, they will have to reexamine certain of their long-held values and beliefs about "doing good," ideals, perhaps utopian, that they have tried their best not to compromise. Thus, in varying degrees of intensity or distress, and at unpredictable points in the educational experience, serious learners are likely to undergo what might be called a crisis of confidence or a loss of innocence. Clearly, it is a critical time that cries for the best a teacher, or mentor, can offer. Such a moment, the ontological moment when reflective and analytic thinking are keenly responsive, provides an opportunity for learning of the highest order. It is the time when the embryonic liberal ironist shows itself.

Two
Social Work Education: History, Structure, Content

Now that we have considered the process of learning, it is time to turn to the principles of learning. In social work education issues such as poverty, ethics, diversity, and empowerment move on and off the front burner of educational priority with regularity depending on what Jerome Bruner (1996) in his recent book calls the "culture of education." Bruner's discussion considers the principles of education from an interesting angle. Culturalism takes account of symbolism and meaning making—how human beings as members of cultures create, transform, and communicate meanings. Clearly, this view redefines the normative roles of teacher and student, practitioner and client who, metaphorically, cannot be speaking the same language given the influence of cultural variations on their respective world views. Bruner's approach presses us to look first at and question the function that education serves in its particular culture, why it is situated in the culture as it is, and how it reflects the distribution of power, status, and other benefits. This suggests the importance of examining the history and culture of the social work profession to discover how educational systems as we now know them have become institutionalized. I will briefly look at the progression of ideas that have shaped the current culture of teaching and learning in social work, giving proper attention to what was at stake politically or ideologically in the emergence of this culture.

To organize my discussion I will borrow a familiar analogy, "the tree of knowledge" (with a nod to that Biblical garden). The roots of this tree include the origins of the profession's ideas and principles about the proper education of social workers—its doctrines and philosophy about requisite knowledge and where and how it should be taught. Its trunk is shaped by the various propositions about and models of social work education that have grown out of the historic roots over the years. A third component of the analogy corresponds to the tree's vital nutrient of knowledge content, or what is expected to be learned. In a manner of speaking, it is this substance that nurtures, invigorates, and complements the philosophical, ideological, and theoretical culture of the tree of teaching and learning. My metaphorical tree is the product of an attempt to weave the diverse threads of the profession's history—in this instance, the ideological, theoretical, and functional—into a semblance of its particular educational design and structure. Like any history of a profession's emergence and development, mine is interpretive and selective.

The Roots—Origins of Social Work Ideas and Principles

The joy of doing history is sharpened by the coincidence that it is within the profession's centennial year that I briefly trace the history of ideas and other cultural influences that brought social work education to where it presently is. I want to do more than merely remap the temporal and factual milestones of social work history. Far more critical are the persuasions and ambitions of personages, the ideology of the times, the variations of power, and the changes in who held it. As already suggested and as observed by Graham (1998), educational programs are often shaped by forces that are not directly based on assumptions about how people learn. Social work education has not escaped these forces.

The last years of the 19th century and the early 20th century mark a significant period of struggle for social work to define itself and its professional function. This period witnessed the fruition of the ideas of the earlier age of Enlightenment. Attention turned from the heart and soul of the Romanticists to the mind and reason of the Modernists and then to the galloping growth of the natural sciences. In the medical profession, already long-established, physicians struggled with the choice between professionalization and democratization. Should they define themselves as practitioners of clinical medicine that treats disease or purveyors of social medicine concerned with prevention? Professionalization, as we know, won out (Starr, 1982). Although the debate in social work was not nearly as vigorous as that in medicine, social work fell in line with the physicians' idea of what a profession should be.

As part of their acceptance of the physicians' definition of a profession, social work embraced a university-affiliated model for education. Adopting this model, the profession eagerly jettisoned its identity as a gentle, feminine vocation by wholeheartedly aligning itself with the assertive masculinity of psychiatric medicine. Elizabeth Lunbeck (1994), in her provocative book, *The Psychiatric Persuasion*, recalls how a prominent psychiatrist lecturing at Smith College in 1918 was impressed by the zeal of his women students who, he was happy to say, did not manifest "the peculiarities of the professional uplifters or reformers" (p. 42). Thus, he could paternalistically pronounce his blessing by granting that indeed there was "room in the world for the social worker." In turn, these generous words inspired his audience of social workers to urge the emerging profession to rule out the "uplifters" and "energetic social reformers," those embarrassingly ardent women whose good intentions were no substitute for the scientific method that serious social work demanded.

In effect, this gender bias was also voiced by Abraham Flexner (2000/1915), whose famous report rationalized and reinforced the increasingly masculine, scientific bent of the profession. He is remembered in the professional literature for his speech, "Is Social Work a Profession?" delivered at the National Conference of Charities and Corrections in 1915, in which he asserted in resoundingly negative terms that social work was not and could not be a profession because it was devoid of science and demonstrable skills. In his words, "A profession is a brotherhood." Lunbeck (1994) observes critically that

> Flexner could imagine "brotherhood" as free of invidious implications, in an arena as highly charged with gender tension as this, only underscores how imperceptible yet significant gender was in the avowedly meritocractic world of the professions. (p. 25)

In another recent book that revisits the early professionalization of social work, Regina Kunzel (1993) examines the liabilities of the profession's turn toward a scientific outlook. She traces the social problem of unmarried mothers at the turn of the century and how quasi-religious and evangelical groups established group homes for these women (the Florence Crittenton Homes, for example) with the aim of redemption and doing good works. In their efforts to professionalize and legitimize their field, female social workers at that time sought to reclaim the treatment of these mothers from the altruistic, amateurish efforts of the evangelicals. However, their application of a framework of rationality and effectiveness, and the subsequent introduction of the language of psychoanalysis, led to the argument that problem girls should be treated in accord with the medical model—specifically by physicians, men, who were presumably more expertly trained. The unintended consequence, Kunzel contends, of the scientific aspirations of social workers was further stigmatization of the already denigrated unmarried mothers as "pathological and criminal," according to the medical diagnostic code. As it turned out, these women professionals proved themselves to be no more objective and free of bias than the evangelical women they disdained.

But as Lunbeck points out, the trajectory from feminine sentiment to masculine science offered immediate rewards. Becoming a professional allowed the social worker to temporarily transcend the social constraints of her gender and move with greater confidence in the male world. As a professional she could attend and deliver lectures, read and write journal articles, and claim and confer the emblems of her professional status. Professionalism gave the female social worker a measure of power and status that the former charity workers never enjoyed. But there also were costs. The professionalism these social workers enjoyed, especially those in the medical and psychiatric fields, had been granted by the higher authority of the predominantly male professions. Therefore, this higher authority could set the standards and conditions governing the roles and functions of social workers.

In sharp contrast, the lure of scientific respectability went unheeded in the professional community of Chicago, the home of the settlement movement. Here, ardent women with good intentions were not dismissed as feminine embarrassments; instead, they conferred upon themselves their own professional authority. Hull House settlement, more than merely a refuge for women (and men) whose college education was scarcely an asset in that era, offered the opportunity to put their training to productive use. As Sklar (1985) explains:

> the social settlement movement supplied perfect structure for women seeking secular means of influencing society because it collectivized their talents, it placed and protected them among the working-class immigrants whose lives demanded amelioration, and it provided them with access to the male political arena while preserving their independence from male-dominated institutions. (pp. 658–667)

Another voice, inflected by the thinking of her colleague and friend, John Dewey, was that of Jane Addams arguing for a method of learning and practice that represented a kind of science derived from direct practice and an understanding of what worked. This was in contrast to more formal scientific studies espoused by the profession. Gender was not the issue, as she wrote in her 1899 essay, "A Function of the Social Settlement":

> At last certain people have consciously formed themselves into groups for the express purpose of effective application. These groups which are called settlements have naturally sought spots where the dearth of this applied knowledge was most obvious, the depressed quarters of great cities. They gravitate to these spots, not with the object of finding clinical material, not to found "sociological laboratories," not indeed with the analytical motive at all, but rather in a reaction from that motive, with a desire to use synthetically and directly whatever knowledge they, as a group, may possess, to test its validity and to discover the conditions under which this knowledge may be employed. (Addams, 1997/1889)

The ideal and developed settlement would attempt to test the value of human knowledge by action and realization, quite as the complete and ideal university would concern itself with the discovery of knowledge in all branches. The settlement stands for application as opposed to research, for emotions as opposed to abstraction, for universal interest as opposed to specialization. Addams defined the artistry of practice, the importance of historic consciousness, social reform, and the development of standards of moral democracy. Ironically, as we will see, there was a true prescience in Addams's beliefs. Without the benefit of modern thought and language, she anticipated the new knowledge about learning and practice that has gained currency in recent years. Her incipient ideas now find more coherent expression in the work of such modern pragmatists and educators as Richard Rorty, Donald Schön, Kieran Egan, Kenneth Gergen, James Bruner, and others .

In some sectors of the profession not entirely bound by the precepts of science, there is a growing appreciation of the central role of the narrative—the client's story (Dean, 1995; Laird, 1989; White & Epston, 1990). From the story of Jane Addams and the settlement movement we can detect the extent to which certain beliefs held as truths by individuals are social constructs; we can appreciate that human circumstances are more deeply known in their social and cultural contexts and their historical perspective, and conclude that commitment to democratic principles and social justice is the bedrock of our work with people. Addams's belief in the values of inductive and experiential learning gained in the active, living field of experience is the leitmotif of her work.

But the advancing tide of professionalism and specialization soon overran the eloquent arguments of Jane Addams and John Dewey. Some universities (including Dewey's home base, the University of Chicago), believing that such views of education and learning were romantic and pre-scientific, not only took increasing control of the development and dissemination of knowledge, but began to branch into an array of distinct fields and disciplines. As Lagemann (1997) recounts, the rigid division between the development and application of knowledge was compounded by the assumption that males were inclined to be inventive and females tended to be intuitive, malleable, nurturing, and caring. In other words, the expectation was that men would generate knowledge and women would apply it. With universities holding a virtual monopoly on knowledge creation, social settlements were redefined as centers for charity or, at best, as laboratories where scholars might go to study and document the problems of the poor and the deviant.

It is interesting to speculate on what the profession, as well as its educational schemes and practices, would look like in the present if Jane Addams's voice were heeded over the academic soundings of university educators. Given the profession's current struggle with its identity and public impressions of social work, would it have made a difference if her humanistic persuasions about the democratic and moral mission of social work had assumed influence over the "scientific methods serious social work demanded" (Addams, 1997/1899, p. 31)?

Oftentimes on interpreting history we tend to read into its twists and quirks our own version of linearity and logic. For instance, I hear an echo of Jane Addams's turn-of-the-century insights in Liane Davis's (1985) article, "Female and Male Voices in Social Work." Drawing from the notable work of Carol Gilligan on the difference between the male and female voice, Davis examines the contemporary rift that has grown between social work academicians who, in her metaphor, speak primarily with male voices and social work practitioners who speak with female voices. Davis's observation that the female voice has been the voice of traditional social work recalls the roles and attitudes of those early settlement workers. In a narrative and contextual frame, the female voice speaks of relationship as the heart of helping people and responsibility and caring as a basic moral principle. The male voice, as Davis hears it, is more abstract and formal, striving for objectivity and individual rights. It is concerned with competence, accountability, and effectiveness, and depends on empirical knowledge about behavior and change. The university where knowledge is discovered and tested is the home of the male voice. The habitat of the female voice is, as Addams once said, the practice field with its emphasis on testing the *value* of human knowledge by action and realization.

But let us not get trapped in this artificial dichotomy, for the idea of female and male voices is, of course, an analogy. It is a means of describing a schism that originated almost a century ago and that has widened in recent years with the growing sophistication of scientific methods. Davis proposes that it is more expedient to speak of two "truths," two versions of understanding and helping. Optimally, the two should complement and support one another. The ambitions of academicians and researchers to develop knowledge and theory would be enhanced if the profession would turn to the field of practice "to capture the phenomenon of treatment-in-action."

The Trunk—Educational Models

Although it is always engaging to look back at "what might have been" in the history of most anything, pragmatic necessities compel us to consider "what could only have been." The turn to a scientific approach to professional social work education in those early years was almost inevitable considering the spirit of the times. The promise of scientific thinking could not be resisted either in medicine or in the newly flourishing social sciences. At the same time, despite the affirmation by the settlement movement of the fundamental mission of social work, its influence on the development of the field was limited from the outset. First, this movement was largely regional, contained for the most part in the Chicago area. Second, although the opportunities and roles it offered educated women (and men) were extraordinary, they fit neither the East coast mandate (forget sentiment and caring and be scientific) for women's entry into the profession, nor social norms governing women's place in society. Thus the educational model that might have emerged from the settlement movement—one that took direct experience with clients as its base—did not take hold. Fortunately, group work preserved the aim for individual fulfillment through democratic participation; until the mid-1930s it functioned somewhat independently of casework, the profession's primary method of social work. And settlement houses and neighborhood centers still operate in many regions and cities.

While the imprint of the settlement movement on systems of professional knowledge and practice was not deep, its effect on the profession as a whole has been lasting. The people and philosophy of the settlement movement persisted over the years, and their activism has carried over in the efforts of contemporary group and community workers and adult educators who continue to remind the mainstream profession of the original mission of social work. They do not let us forget that the "work" of social work is in the streets and neighborhoods, in reform, in advocacy for the marginal and disenfranchised, and in the importance of democratic action and education.

Kunzel (1993), like Davis (1985) sees the domination of the profession by a particular gender-based ideology as leading to the current state of affairs. However, she also suggests that it could not have been otherwise, considering the tremendous compulsion (from within and without) to "defeminize" the profession. She notes:

> Extolling the virtues of efficiency, objectivity, and expertise, social work leaders disparaged the values aligned with nineteenth-century benevolence as overly sentimental, embarrassingly anachronistic, and suggestive of professional immaturity. In condemning the qualities of emotion, sentiment, and intuition, social workers occasionally gave way to a more explicit rejection of earlier benevolence as excessively feminine. (p. 44–45)

The abandonment of social work's philanthropic origins, from what he called "cause" to "function," was given official sanction by Porter Lee in his presidential address to the National Conference on Social Welfare in 1929. Announcing that social workers had entered a new era, he advised them to turn their attention from social evils to internal professional demands. "Cause," he said, called for "zeal," the "flaming spirit," whereas "function" demanded "intelligence," "standards and methods," and "efficient personnel" (p. 5). The trained technician rather than the crusader was the ideal social worker. But despite the travails that "defeminization" of the profession galvanized, it also offered women certain benefits. Nancy Cott (1987) tells us that the existence of ascertainable standards, rather than subjective criteria for training and achievement, meant that women could strive to meet those standards and proceed as if they were to be judged as individuals, rather than being judged a priori on account of sex.

The establishment of training schools was the natural consequence of the push for professionalization. Early in the century these schools were not affiliated with academic institutions, but developed out of the small staff training programs in voluntary social agencies. Teachers were selected from the groups of practitioners rather than faculty holding advanced degrees in the theoretical social sciences; it was believed that practitioners could offer learners the benefits of their extensive experience. Students were trained for direct service or casework in host organizations, including general and psychiatric hospitals, child guidance clinics, and public schools. But as the number of university based schools of social work grew (influenced in part by the ascendance of Freudian theory), field work was increasingly split off from the academic classroom.

From early in the 20th century onward, field instruction occupied a curious and ambiguous role in the overall educational scheme. In moving from an apprenticeship model of education to a professional model, educators presumed that classroom courses should provide the essential body of social work knowledge and principles. This acquired knowledge would guide learning in the field where students were expected to acquire specific practice skills. The result has been a persistent dichotomy instead of a functional partnership between class and field in many schools. The progression of this educational structure has not been without its critics. Over the years some of the profession's noteworthy leaders have voiced their concerns. Although they were mainstream educators who accepted the prevailing assumptions about learning and the separation of class and field, the legacy of these leaders rests on their expressed belief that learning should be holistic, responsive to the needs of students, and ultimately a relational process and experience.

In 1931 Edith Abbott, then dean of the School of Social Service Administration at the University of Chicago, wrote that social work should emulate medical education by offering both academic and clinical training. However, she qualified this stiff structural division by explaining that in her university academic and clinical teachers often were one and the same. Since clinical teachers of medicine were members of the academic faculty, medical students experienced a sense of continuity between the theories and practice of their profession. Noting that the provision of adequate field work and its educational organization was the most difficult aspect of social work education, she pleaded for greater unity between class and field so that one might serve to strengthen the other.

Eleven years later, Bertha Reynolds in her classic work, *Learning and Teaching in the Practice of Social Work* (1942), also complained that close relations between the school, with its responsibility for class teaching, and the field agency, with its responsibility for its community function, were hard to maintain. The result is the still unsettled problem of integration of knowledge and practice. As Reynolds put it, students are expected to integrate what they get from class and field, without much help from either. This effort can be further impeded when the concepts learned in class and those learned in the field are contradictory.

Reynolds considered learning an art. Learning, in her view, was something more than an intellectual process: it was an experience involving the whole person. Her words recall John Dewey's appraisal of experience as the medium for closing the gap between knowing and doing. Reynolds (1942) believed that classroom learning could not anticipate real life events. As she put it, even in the course of practice "there are puzzling discrepancies between what teachers and learners expect and what actually happens" (pp. 69–70). The humanistic qualities that enlighten her ideas of teaching and learning are most evident when she cautions teachers to be guided by what is happening to the learner rather than by what they themselves want to accomplish. For her, education was not merely preparation for professional practice, but preparation for living.

Charlotte Towle (1954), practitioner, educator, and humanist, is known for her authoritative book on education for social work, *The Learner in Education for the Professions as Seen in the Education for Social Work*. Early in the book, Towle underscores the idea that learning is not restricted to training or the classroom but is induced through concomitant life experiences: "The practice of social work is inextricably related to the life-experiences of the learner so that it is impossible to isolate the learning experience for study of its effects" (p. 24). In this regard, Towle suggests that learners bring to the educational experience the potential for growth (and regression), their emotional and survival needs, and the indications of how they define self and past experiences.

Towle calls for coordination of the many relationships through which the student learns. She portrays the school as an organic whole comprised of three concentric circles that revolve around the student. The innermost circle represents the field experience; this is encircled by classroom instruction, which, in turn, is encompassed by the school as an institution (pp. 138–139). At the center, within a student's field experience is her relationship with her field instructor, which, as Towle argues, is the most crucial relationship in enabling the student to respond to the immediate demands of practice and put new learning to use. The middle circle embraces the student's relationship with classroom instructors, but only if instructors are able to talk *with* rather than talk *to* students, "engaging them deeply for and against their thinking." The third circle is the school as an institution, but again, only if the administration encourages student participation rather than remaining remote and threatening as the top authority to which the student is accountable. Towle's paradigm anticipates what we now know as crucial to the development of professional competence and integrity, that is, the pivotal significance of mentorship, the relationship between field teacher and learner (Schön, 1983, 1987).

Yet another educational authority shared Towle's concern about the incongruence of field and class and her attempt to resolve it. Coincident with her book was the 1951 publication of *Social Work Education in the United States*, a study done for the National Council on Social Work Education. Better known as the Hollis-Taylor report, the authors, Ernest V. Hollis and Alice L. Taylor, were officials of the Federal Security Agency. The purpose of the study was to build a framework of principles within which existing social work programs might be examined to establish a structure for the accreditation of acceptable programs. However, in contrast to the work of Abbott or Reynolds and Towle, this study only served to further solidify (if not petrify) the trunk of social work education. Where Towle dismissed the notion of curricular "portions" or divisions, the authors of the Hollis-Taylor report based their work on the controversial assumption that class and field were products of innately different educational traditions and thus deserved to be separate entities (pp. 230–231).

Beyond the different traditions, Hollis and Taylor implied that class and field represented different educational values. Where field instruction was rooted in an apprenticeship type of education, classroom instruction had its roots in the traditions of American higher education. Moreover, each type of education was seen as representing "deep-lying differences in purpose and philosophy." In their view, classroom instruction centered on the body of social work knowledge, principles, and other theories that give order and meaning to practice. In contrast, field education tended "to center largely on specific knowledge and skills."

Hollis and Taylor proposed certain practical and structural changes in field education. They recommended, for example, increasing the status and compensation for field instructors, reconsidering the amount of time required in field education, and clarifying its purposes, objectives, and content. Added almost as an afterthought, the authors referred to a faculty member's thoughtful words: "Little will be achieved in remedying details until we decide whether field work is primarily motivating, maturing, interest-sustaining, attitude-influencing, illustrating, implementing, skill-generating, or some blend of these and other objectives" (p. 234)

Study of the Council on Social Work Education (CSWE) Curriculum Policy Statement (CPS) current at this writing shows just how well the trunk of education has been shaped and cultivated over the decades following the Hollis-Taylor report. The CPS advises that the field practicum, as an integral component of the curriculum in social work education, "engages the student in supervised social work practice and provides opportunities to apply classroom learning in the field setting" (CSWE, 1992, M6.14).

In this statement the "knowing-understanding-doing" paradigm of learning remains firm and intact, as does its ideological foundation. As the CPS puts it, "Every part of the master's curriculum must strengthen the student's understanding and appreciation of a scientific, analytic approach to building knowledge for the delivery and evaluation of practice" (CSWE, 1992, M6.2). Together these statements support the teaching model of education described at the outset of this monograph. As the reader may recall, the teaching model is top-down, didactic, and deductive. It occurs in conventional classroom settings where knowledge is passed along in an organized fashion with the aim of achieving certain preordained objectives.

The Nutrients—Educational Content

Clearly, the structure of anything must be related in some way to what it contains or supports. Or in more familiar terms, form follows function. It is obvious that the structure of an educational system is designed to provide a systematic way of conveying knowledge of some kind to learners. But it seems reasonable to assume that the knowledge to be conveyed should determine the nature of an educational structure and not the other way around. New systems of teaching science in universities and high schools called "inquiry-based," "discovery," or plain "hands-on learning," make the center of learning the lab or field, rather than the traditional classroom. These new systems are based on emerging assumptions about how people learn and the kinds of knowledge (in large part, experiential) that might be acquired through this approach.

The structure of social work education has persisted with some variations on a uniform theme. To be sure, ambitious efforts have been undertaken to rework the structure. These efforts have addressed time factors, measures for achieving greater integration, the varied use and timing of field placements, the roles of field instructors, and so on. New windows on the world, theories and constructs, have been introduced, scrapped, or replaced. But the structure or paradigm of social work education has generally remained intact. It seems to me that one compelling reason for the persistence of this teaching model is the kind of knowledge that this model was designed to convey—namely theories, methods, and skills that could be taught in a didactic and prescriptive manner. In other words, the educational program was (and still is) a honeycomb of courses to equip students with what it has been believed they ought to know and understand to work with people. Although other professions use similar teaching models, social work over time has been unique in terms of the remarkable inconsistency of its subject matter (see Goldstein, 1973).

The wellspring of developing theory in social work was, of course, Mary Richmond's *Social Diagnosis* (1917). The book at once achieved many purposes. It answered Flexner's criteria for social work's acceptance into the "brotherhood" of professions and, in effect, became the bible that social work needed to move from the apprenticeship model of training in the field to professional education in the classroom. Richmond's work cleared the way for the profession's embrace of psychoanalytic theory, then coming around the bend. Where *Social Diagnosis* organized the procedures and system of practice, psychoanalytic theory provided the grand and eloquent rationale for practice. It also succeeded in shifting the focus of practice from contextual (societal and communal) explanations of causality to intrapsychic ones. In the following years, the deterministic principles of Freudian psychology shaped the conventions and form of the profession's knowledge base and came to be known as the Diagnostic school. Among others of that time, Bertha Reynolds (1942) was troubled that the profession was losing sight of its commitments to the whole person, to the community, and to reform.

In the first of a series of shifts that attempted to revamp the rationale for professional practice, another school of practice emerged in the 1930s, the Functional school of social work. Its origins were neither scientific nor academic, but the result of psychologist Jesse Taft's experience in analytic treatment with Otto Rank, one of a number of defectors from Freud's classic psychoanalysis. Taft (1935) and Virginia Robinson (1930) turned the Freudian Diagnostic school on its head by replacing scientism with their notions of humanism. Determinism was out; will and free choice became the new catchwords, at least in some graduate social work programs. With the helping relationship as the medium for growth and change, the client was not perceived as the product of life's previous circumstances, but someone who could change in the here and now by the conscious use of will. Concepts of diagnosis, pathology, and cure were repudiated by the emphasis on growth and becoming, the projected outcomes of the Functionalist approach. Thus the knowledge base didn't exactly grow but split into two forms, each filling the "what to teach" needs of particular programs. But the estrangement of the two methods and schools was short lived. By the end of World War II, the crisp borders between the Functional and Diagnostic schools began to relax. Doctrinaire Freudian psychology was easing into a more secular ego psychology, and the growing number of schools of social work were juggling and combining various approaches.

In the optimistic glow of the postwar years, the maturing social sciences offered the promise that long-troubling social problems might finally be remedied through the use of sophisticated scientific research methods. Social work eagerly grasped this hope and supplemented course content with new theories and methods of inquiry. My doctoral studies in the early 1960s were heavily seasoned with an assortment of role theories, the use of chi squared and other quantitative recipes, and something called non-parametric statistics. But a few isolated thinkers were not entirely convinced about the promise of the social sciences and took up the cause of humanism. They contended that science could furnish means but not ends, instruments but not goals, facts but not values. Reliance on the superficialities of science and its methods, rather than on an adequate understanding of the human condition, would result in the loss of the profession's vitality (see Lindemann, 1949; Stroup, 1960).

Just a quick glance at the late 1960s and early 1970s suggests an anthropological expedition into a realm of occult religions (although, to be sure, most were variations on or antidotes to the scriptures of Freudianism). Gurus and high priests, psychotherapists who transformed their personal styles and methods into "schools, " charismatically spread their word through workshops and books. Social work practice teachers could choose Carl Rogers's client-centered doctrines, Eric Berne's transactional analysis, Albert Ellis's rational-emotive therapy, William Glasser's reality therapy, Fritz Perls's gestalt therapy, and Arthur Janov's primal scream therapy, among others. There were group therapies of all kinds: marathon, psychodrama, and T-groups. There were also family therapies to fit any notion of how families worked or what they needed. These included intergenerational therapy, structural therapy, communicational therapy, crisis therapy, role therapy, and others. For the most part, these therapies were comprised of an aggregation of dramatic techniques and strategies of the prescriptive, "how-to-do" variety, with scarce reference to a substantial supportive theory.

How was it that these theories and methods were so readily absorbed by so many social work programs? The most obvious reason is that such techniques and skills are easy to teach and delightful to learn, especially when there were masters who could dramatically spotlight their therapeutic wares. But another reason was the ongoing dichotomy between classroom and field instruction, between the knowing and doing of education. Curriculum planners and classroom teachers had the license to teach what seemed to them appropriate for the preparation of students for professional practice, without reference to the realities of practice in the field. Coincidentally, social agencies and field centers were complicit with this educational scheme by calling for schools to produce students armed with similarly aligned skills and technique for direct practice. Ann Hartman (1990), for example cites the sharply critical 1972 position statement of the Family Service Association of America, which called for schools of social work to equip their graduates with more practice techniques and skills. It is worth noting that the complaint became louder in the following years when many schools adopted a generalist curriculum. Agencies that provided very specialized services protested that graduates of generalist programs were not equipped with the required expertise (Goldstein, 1981a).

Of even greater significance in answering the question of social work's absorption of popular theories and methods on helping is the absence of an overarching epistemological outlook. As the various helping approaches gained popularity, educators had no epistemological reference point from which they could begin to question and reflect on the assumptions, foundations, and validity of the knowledge and methods they were teaching.

The current Curriculum Policy Statement tacitly grants parity to all theories and methods that fit (the criteria are unclear) into "the common body of knowledge, values, and skills of the profession," yet it seems to favor deterministic or causal explanations of the human condition. Statements such as "the bio-psycho-social variables that affect individual development of behavior," or "the ways in which systems promote or deter people in the maintaining or achieving optimal health and well-being" express this bias toward determinism. Whether inquiry is focused on intergenerational frictions, structural dysfunctions of the family, role conflicts, poor object relations, transference problems, or other causal forces, the findings of such inquiry are questionable. My esteemed colleague, Prof. Edmund Sherman says this more eloquently:

> In the complex realm of human affairs this causal thinking can be heavy-handed and potentially destructive. . . . Behind it is the hubris that we can fix anything. There are things we can't fix because we can't go back to the condition that presumably "caused" the problem, since the sequellae have taken on a complicated life of their own. (personal communication, August 3, 1998)

Such simplistic "cause-and-effect" thinking augments the license of the educator to select from the array of corresponding theories and methods, thereby enhancing the authority and autonomy of the academic classroom in its relation to its poor cousin, field instruction.

Altogether, the shift from the apprenticeship model of social work education to the dominance of university-based programs may have increased concern about the class-field dichotomy, but it did not succeed in narrowing it. From the 1970s on the adoption by educators of the social systems and the eco-systems models as schemes for conceptualizing the complexities of person-context relations, has further strengthened the intellectual authority of the classroom. Despite their limitations, the social work practice courses that were in vogue prior to the adoption of the systems model (the methods classes called casework, group work, and community organization) did have the value of serving as implicit links with the field. In effect, class and field shared similar orientations to practice; theories of casework taught in class had practice analogues in the field. This continuum was harder to maintain when the abstractions of high-level systems theory were adopted for classroom instruction. Concepts such as "macro-mezzo-micro" or "generalist" didn't quite fit the pragmatics of the field. That field instructors had to be retaught these theories and vocabulary further strengthened the hand of the academy.

The increasing amount of content to teach, which was itself increasingly abstract, did not help to lessen the distance between class and field. If there were any spaces in the trunk of knowledge, the curriculum, they soon overflowed with the intricacies of a theory that really had no direct application in real-life practice. I discovered this while trying to teach the unitary or systems approach I helped introduce into our program and subsequently wrote about and published on. The compelling and attractive theory is, after all, a conceptual structure that enables the observer to arbitrarily create some hypothetical relationships among people and circumstances. While I could cover the classroom blackboards with an impressive complex of interlocking circles and double-pointed arrows, none of the diagrams contained a hint of what to do. We might deduce *where* in the system the most "effective intervention" should occur, but not *how to* intervene (recall, this was the basis of the complaint of the agencies looking for professionals with more skills than lenses).

The intellectual authority of the academy, as distinct from the field, has grown in another way. Increasingly, social work literature has come to represent the views of academics in a booming textbook industry. If one browses the practice-oriented journal *Social Casework* (renamed *Families in Society* in 1990) one will find that in the 1950s and 1960s articles written by agency administrators, supervisors, and practitioners occupied a fair share of most issues. One could read about such topics as casework in a family court, family sessions in foster care, and the many issues in supervision and agency functions. Certainly, these first-hand accounts of practice and its many dimensions had some influence on service and education. Together these accounts served as a forum within which professionals in the field could share such experiences. These articles were also useful teaching tools. As assigned readings, the experiences and reflections of seasoned social worker practitioners helped students to vicariously learn what social work was really like. Now, as the editor of *Families in Society*, I find that commentaries on direct practice are authored mainly by academics in the form of research reports or theoretical articles; professionals who confront the stark actualities of practice in the field are virtually silent.

On review, the analogy of the tree of knowledge serves to portray the organic nature and growth of social work education. The shift from a humanistic, philanthropic prospect to the promise of scientific methods was deeply rooted in the ideological ground of the profession's early years. More than an ideational change, this shift represented a change in values and mission from cause to function and a move from an apprenticeship model of education to a university based system. Significant in its own special way was the transformation, as Kunzel (1993) says, from a "women's occupation to a true profession" (p. 48). She explains that women "hoped to de-gender the act of helping, to transform it from a religious, feminine calling into a profession worthy of broad respect, legitimacy, and remuneration." Securing the secular authority of a scientifically based professionalism had its consequences. As Kunzel suggests, "by joining their male colleagues in posing professionalism and femininity as mutually exclusive, however, [women] participated in the process of gendering professionalism in a way that equated professionalism with masculinity." Together, these shifts from women's work to profession, humanism to science, led to a conventional academic educational structure in which the classroom was (and, of course, still is) the preeminent source of learning. The "knowing-understanding-doing" prototype of learning, a top-down, deductive approach, became the standard of professional education. Field education, by design a bottom-up, inductive medium of learning, assumed a secondary role, and an insistently vexing dichotomy has evolved.

Points of View on the Field-Classroom Relationship

Listening to students, recalling one's own formative years as a student, and observing the linkages (or their absence) between class and field stir doubt about the presumed hierarchy of class over field and the linear progression of the learning process. As Donald Schön (1987) says, even in the applied sciences the reflective and artistic talents of the learner and practitioner mediate the relation of knowledge to practice.

Schön's premise that a practitioner's skill is not restricted to expertise in theory and technique, that each unique situation calls for a new theory, was illustrated for me recently. Telephone company technicians came to my home to try to locate the "line noise" that was disrupting the effectiveness of my computer's modem. Bearing computers and other testing devices, they quickly ruled out any major problems. Among themselves, the technicians exchanged ideas, probabilities, and past experiences. Nothing applied. The metaphor "reflection-in-action" was almost visible when they mulled, stared at an imagined diagram, shook their heads, and like explorers narrowed their search to a remote splice that had somehow degraded. Like archaeologists discovering a new artifact, they grinned. When I praised their genius, they modestly shrugged saying, "Just common sense."

Is working with people and the degraded splices in their lives fundamentally different? Of course, the perversity and contradictions are of an even higher order, and complexity and exceptions to the norm are commonplace. The kind of teaching and learning that prepares practitioners for such contingencies will turn out to be circuitous or even spiral-like. Often the spark of a solution might be a seemingly innocuous comment remembered from an interview, a sleepless moment's insight, or a momentary digression by a teacher. Learning may be planned but, as I mentioned earlier, if didactic models and theories prematurely structure it, the opportunities that arise for reflection might be overlooked.

Where does field instruction, the practicum in its own right, fit into the evolution of social work education's design? In his study of the history of field instruction, George Aase (1982) records the great variance across the years in arrangements for field instruction. The number of hours required in the field has varied, as has use of concurrent, block, or combined field placements and use of field seminars. Agencies used for placements have varied widely in their orientations and in their programs. Subsequently, "articulation of learning activities between class and field" became the desired goal based on the enduring assumption that primary responsibility for educational design should reside in the academy. With the support of governmental grants, various experiments were launched including shifting social work classes to the field, creating community based field-teaching centers, and designing field units to focus on social problems rather than method (aging, poverty, or disability, for example).

Currently, although opinions vary a great deal, there appears to be no question about the primacy of the classroom. Sheafor and Jenkins (1982) call for the "articulated approach," or a planned relationship between cognitive and experiential learning. They say that "it has the purpose of linking classroom learning with practice activities so that the new social worker can effectively engage in knowledge and value-guided practice" (p. 4). But they sadly note that while this has long been a goal, the planned linkage rarely occurs on paper and even more rarely in practice. They express regret that field instruction has not received the disciplined attention it deserves, that experiential education has not truly developed academic credibility, and that research and scholarship to strengthen this form of teaching have been given relatively little attention (p. xi).

Gayla Rogers (1996), a director of field education, has similar regrets, adding that studies have shown problems such as the inadequate supply of placements, the inconsistency in learning opportunities, and the turnover of field instructors. Her most telling criticism, however, eclipses these flaws. Her study of the teaching methods of fields instructors (Rogers & McDonald, 1995) found that these instructors did not subscribe to any formal approach to field education but instead used whatever teaching methods were expedient in producing students who were ready for beginning professional practice. Because of role strain and time constraints, they relied on methods that were most effective and least time consuming from their point of view. Rogers and McDonald also found that less attention is given to the actual development and operationalization of field education theories and models than to writing about them.

Bogo and Vayda's book, *The Practice of Field Instruction in Social Work* (1998), offers a second perspective from the field. Speaking mainly to an audience of field instructors, the authors not only subscribe to the existing curricular scheme, but raise the principle of separating class and field to a higher level of conceptualization. In their view, class and field are indeed distinct educational entities, each operating within its respective frame of reference. The school is responsible for education, knowledge-building, teaching, and research, whereas the field is concerned with service, effectiveness, and efficiency. A hierarchical note is sounded in their assumption that the term "faculty" applies only to university based teachers. Field instructors are, well, field instructors. Although the authors' model of education focuses primarily on the practicum itself, it is similar to the knowing-understanding-doing formula of learning. To this formula the authors' model adds the dimension of "reflection," which includes the social worker's personal and subjective abilities. Although this educational model advances and marks out the responsibilities of the practicum, at the same time it reinforces the divide between academic and experiential learning. Further, it places total control of the educational process in the university.

Concerns about the lack of proper attention, research, or effort in improving the quality of field education carry with them the unspoken implication that with proper attention, research, and effort the problem might be fixed. I don't think this is possible.

There are inherent flaws in the current educational model, among them the problems that derive from the structure of the model itself. Directors of field instruction strive to maintain the integrity of the structure and, at the same time, narrow the gap that exists between class and field. Theirs is a Sisyphean task. How does one succeed in articulating—even keeping up with—what is being taught in the classrooms that, themselves, vary so much in content, philosophy, and the special perspective of the teacher? In turn, if it were possible to translate the cognitive content of the classroom into the world of practice, consider the challenge in attempting to articulate this knowledge with the variable nature of the social agencies in which students are placed. They differ considerably in terms of function, time, and opportunities afforded students to gain the needed experience.

Thus, it is not surprising that field instructors, as Rogers found, see the realities of practice in less than harmonious ways. Classroom teachers tend to hold an abstract view of learning, based on models, theories, and research that open new horizons for effective change. Field instructors, in contrast, deal with the exigencies of the immediate moment, the pressing demands of real-life cases, the task that must be accomplished in the here and now. It is a rough comparison indeed, but it is not dissimilar to the difference between the poet in the ivory tower and the laborer in the field. Should such structural obstacles be hurdled, two other factors suggest the need for a new educational system. One factor concerns the growing new knowledge and understanding about human behavior and change; the other has to do with what we are beginning to comprehend about how people learn. The two factors are by no means mutually exclusive since the question of learning is reciprocally tied to human behavior. Let me briefly summarize these ideas since they will be the targets of inquiry in the forthcoming section of this book.

The Dualities of Learning

Contemporary knowledge about the complexities and vagaries of human behavior and human change leads to a reframing of a critical question. Rather than asking *what* we need to understand about the human condition, we must now ask *how* we begin to understand and make sense of that condition. The first question is based on the assumption that there are normative matrices or frameworks within which we can organize and explain data about a particular human event; the second lays this assumption to rest. Much of the normative knowledge about human behavior and change can be taught didactically. Frameworks (e.g., types of psychopathology), theories (e.g., psychodynamic), and models of practice (e.g., various approaches to family therapy) can be transmitted in an instructive if not prescriptive fashion. This kind of knowledge answers the question of *what* needs to be learned. The question of *how* we understand the human condition, *generative* knowledge, does not lend itself to didactic forms of teaching and learning.

As Saleebey (1998) explains, where normative knowledge is deductive, abstract, conservative, and prescriptive, generative knowledge is inductive and open-ended. By its nature, generative knowledge engages a curious, reflective, and inquiring mind that questions conventional assumptions about person and society and that seeks fresh and dependable alternatives. Feminist and social constructionist theories are but two examples of the generative agenda. To put it simply, generative theories are action theories that are best taught in the real-life world, not the isolated classroom that calls on intellect. These and other generative theories are not *about* something but rather *derive from* and are, in turn, applied to the actual lived experience. In effect, learning itself is an experience that, by its nature, is generative, constantly in process, always branching into unforeseen pathways, tripping over the ironies of living, and often guided by whatever artistic and imaginative talents we possess.

In drawing this section of the book to a close, it is important to credit the few leaders who, in their own terms, share this concern for the status, quality, and role of field instruction. Hamilton and Else (1983), for example, speak to what they call a humanist orientation to adult education. They place the learner at the center of the educational process and underscore the importance of respect for learners' dignity and worth. They go on to argue for learners' ability to be self-directed and for the value of their life experiences in making learning both meaningful and effective. They advocate a decreasing emphasis on the transmittal techniques of traditional teaching and increasing emphasis on experiential approaches that tap the experience of the learners and involve them in the analysis and meaning of that experience.

In his reflections on the centennial year of field education in social work and the approaching millennial year, Dean Schneck (1991) comments on the challenges that lie ahead. Referring to the maturation of the profession, Schneck notes the shift from an apprenticeship approach to the centralization and control of knowledge development in the university. He proposes that in the future it is possible that knowledge building will become the responsibility of both school and field, given that new problems and emerging human needs are more typically confronted in the field. More specifically he notes that

> in the future, field education could become the primary medium for the bridge between the university function to generate and disseminate knowledge and innovation (the educational ideal) and the professional function to apply and refine knowledge in specific practice applications (the practice reality).

Schneck adds that if we wish practitioners to be prepared to participate in knowledge building efforts, such experiences should become a part of field teaching and learning. He gives special weight to practice wisdom, the form of learning that can only be achieved in the field.

Echoing some of the themes in the preceding pages, Mesbur and Glassman's (1991) reflections on the dilemmas facing social work field education indirectly support the agenda of experiential learning discussed in the balance of this work. After outlining the rational principles that should guide the field instruction component—integration, faculty commitment, and mutuality—the authors also recognize the need to shift from the ideal to the real when they delineate four dilemmas that block the realization of these thoughtful principles.

They note first the ambivalence that exists within the field about humanistic education and experiential learning. The preoccupation with quality control compels a rush to judgment and evaluation that abandons humanistic principles as if, as they put it, "humanistic educational principles negate standards of excellence." The second dilemma reflects old habits of teaching and supervision rooted in the Diagnostic school. These habits pertain to the control of the student or the expectation that students ought to pattern their approach to practice on their field instructor's. At risk is the learner's integrity and potential creativity. The third dilemma is the lack of a systematic epistemology of knowledge for the profession, a lack of understanding of how or why we select our knowledge for education and practice. The result is the gap between our espoused theories and the assumptions that guide the actualities of practice. The fourth dilemma is the lack of understanding of how practice is performed in the practice world. This dilemma will not be resolved, they assert, until we begin to use a new lens molded by an experiential educational process.

Before proceeding to consider how these questions and dilemmas will serve as compass points for some new directions in professional education, I think it is important to ask why these issues have not risen to the surface in the minds of educational planners. The answer might very well be that either acceptable alternatives did not present themselves or, most likely, if they did, the cost of change and the kinds of revisions and study required to implement it would threaten to be too high. The result has been a short-sighted and repetitive insistence on running the same track. Perhaps unfairly, this disposition brings to mind Paul Watzlawick's (1978) acerbic observation on human single-mindedness: If what you are doing isn't working, do more of it.

The heart of the matter is the way in which dualistic ways of thinking infiltrate the rationale, structure, and content of social work education and, thus, tend to perpetuate the paradigm or system we have considered thus far. To put this another way, most systems of thought and practice hold at their core certain implicit or explicit assumptions about the real world. Among them is the ready tendency to distinguish between certain conditions and states of being when, in fact, they are interrelated or are points on a continuum. This is an assumption inherited from the ancient Platonic distinction between the real and the ideal or the Cartesian distinction between inner thought and external substance. It is apparent when we speak of the dualities of mind and body, facts and values, or moral principles such as good and evil. Certain dualities or discontinuities impede the natural flow of learning and education. First I will consider the distinctions made between art and science; then I will look at the distinctions made between theory and practice. Collectively and individually these two dualities tend to buttress the view of class and field as two distinct educational modalities. For this reason it is important to consider the art/science and theory/practice dualities more fully.

Although the terms art and science are often uttered in the same breath, more often they are thought of as distinct and even incompatible entities, and sometimes one is valued over the other. If false dichotomy means anything, it applies to the distinction between art and science. In the words of the author Raymond Chandler:

> There are two kinds of truth; the truth that lights the way and the truth that warms the heart. The first of these is science, and the second is art. Without art science would be as useless as a pair of high forceps in the hands of a plumber. Without science, art would become a crude mess of folklore and emotional quackery.

Art and science are interdependent; they complement one another. Where science transforms the specific experience into a general form—a law, a principle of practice, or a theoretical supposition—art transforms general experience into a single, unique form (Weiskopf, 1979).

We see the division between art and science played out in recent social work debates about the primacy of the scientific method, specifically in the position that only empirically supported methods of treatment should be provided to our clients. Suspicious as I am of most facile answers, let us say that there is merit and good will in the arguments of Myers and Thyer (1997) who, along with many others, espouse this premise. Let us say that treatment *x* has been subject to countless clinical trials and in relation to depression has by some scale or quantitative measure proven to be whatever "effective" is supposed to represent. It is important to note that one element of the equation is unstated. No matter how strong statistical proof of the effectiveness of the treatment may be, ultimately the treatment is applied, not by a statistical unit, but by a unique human being who happens to be a social worker. To be sure, he or she might apply the treatment with consummate skill. But who is to say that he or she might not be the "plumber with high forceps in his hands"? Irrespective of its objective and empirical qualities, even as a well-tested technique, the method will necessarily be modified or modulated by the interpersonal exchange in which it is enacted. Artistry makes itself known when any method is applied in the personal style of a subjective, mindful helper who is sensitive to the emotional climate and the countless nuances and tinges that configure the special human situation. If this is not the case, what then is social work practice?

Like art and science, theory and practice tend to be thought of as distinct from each other. One refers to thinking, the other to doing. But in the real world of experience, they are inseparable and interdependent. If there is a gap, it exists between the theorist and the practitioner, not between theory and practice. The standard model of professional education does little to bridge this gap, as I have already noted. If only in terms of structure and geographical distance, the separation of class and field sustains the perceived difference between the academician and the practitioner. The university based scholar and educator's stock in trade is creating, analyzing, and disseminating theoretical generalizations *about* knowledge and practice. Somewhere else, in the hurly-burly of field agencies, hospitals, correctional centers, and the like, field instructors are embroiled in the daily rounds of mentoring, the always urgent needs of clients, or the operations of a vulnerable institution. As previously mentioned, studies show that field instructors' concern is with efficiency and effectiveness in getting the job done, in surviving uncompromising schedules and the demands of teaching. They, like academicians, rely on theoretical knowledge, but theirs is of a different order—practice wisdom, perhaps. This kind of theory is not just *about* practice, but also *of* the authentic practice experience. Obviously, one kind of knowledge should inform the other. More accurately (and instrumentally), as I will argue, the experiential knowledge of the field should inform the theoretical knowledge of the classroom.

Of course there should be ongoing colloquies between university based and field based educators. But the most vital medium, or, metaphorically, the synapse, that connects theory and practice is the learner. I think this rather innocent reflection on her placement by a student says this nicely:

> The interviewing style and skills for interviewing are very different from those I learned in my "Interpersonal" courses. The interviews [with my clients] seem intrusive and interrogative in comparison with the soft, gentle methods practiced in class. I have struggled with this approach but realize the style is necessary to obtain relevant information. Also, I found that clients dictate the interview style.

Here the student is commenting on ways that the pressures in the field and the personality, life experience, and needs of the client shape the interview. The freedom in class to be gentle is lost in the field—yet both are important. The student, traveling between the two learning sites, struggles with the difference and often does so alone. How can the teacher in the classroom become more responsive to the student's experience of the field and help the student learn how to respond to the urgencies of the field experience?

Part Two

Learning and Experience

Three
Experiential Learning: Foundations, Constraints, Opportunities

Louis Menand (1997), scholar and educator, tells us:

> People become educated: you can't really stop them. Those who make a profession of educating others believe (against some evidence to the contrary) that it is possible to intervene in that process, or to participate in that process, in ways that are helpful, rather than redundant, counterproductive, or futile. They believe that there are educational outcomes that are more or less desirable, and methods of achieving those outcomes that are more or less effective. But education requires us to deal with singularities, not regularities—to deal with persons, not laboratory models of persons—so we can never be entirely sure in the abstract what will work in the specific case. (p. 1)

If we attach any credibility to Menand's advice, two points become apparent. First, we are indeed talking about the education of a true singularity. That singularity is someone who intends to be a social worker, someone who on any given day will confront the unexpected, often arcane, and singular conditions that contour any one human life. Even more daunting, this someone will try to help people in need—a homeless mother, a grandparent burdened with the care of a disabled grandchild, or tenants facing the adversities of run-down public housing. At the same time, this same person must be responsive to the social context in which these conditions are embedded. Both with knowledge and beyond knowledge, what does this caring helper need to muster to make a difference?

This question leads to the second point. Menand seems to doubt whether it is possible to intervene or participate in the process of education in ways that are helpful. I have suggested that his doubts are warranted, offering examples of students who succeeded in their learning *despite* some very doubtful (albeit, well-meaning) educational interventions. And I have also proposed that social work is in many important ways an art. How does one teach an art? I raise these issues as part of my introduction to the admittedly complex exposition of experiential learning that will follow. The multifarious nature of social work and the versatility required of the social work practitioner, planner, and administrator promise that there is no one inclusive way of teaching. I hope that my discourse on experiential learning will inspire thoughts about the creativity, imagination, and art involved in teaching and learning.

At the outset of this book I proposed that experiential learning and its major context, the practicum, are the integral components of education for professional practice. In a manner of speaking, experiential learning is an example of the concept of "person in the situation." Experiential learning is a kind of learning that focuses on the "learner in the situation." It is in the field where learners confront the real-life circumstances of their clients and thereby begin to integrate the two elements of learning, the knowledge derived from experience with the knowledge generated by theory and research. Noting that its early roots can be found in the philosophy of the settlement house movement and the doctrines of Jane Addams, I have discussed how experiential learning serves to link theory and practice or, more accurately, practice with theory. It is now time to examine the principles of learning, education, and knowledge development articulated by various contemporary thinkers that, together, will form the firm foundation of experiential learning.

The Foundations of Experiential Learning

The actual foundation for learning is memory passed down through the generations. Israeli biologist Yadin Dudai (as cited in

Weiner, 1999) tells us:

> For us to learn anything at all, we must already know a lot. We have to know how to live to know how to learn. Our ability to learn and remember is itself a memory. . . the memory of a discovery passed down from generation to generation since near the beginning of life. . . . Of all the discoveries living things have acquired in their 3.5 billion-year tenure on the Earth, the mnemonic device of memory itself is one of the most crucial. For an individual to profit from his experience and carry each experience forward to the next choice point is one of the most useful adaptations ever evolved. (pp. 132–133)

Clearly, experiential learning in its many forms, is by no means a breakthrough or innovation of any kind. The idea is truly vintage John Dewey and, by affiliation, Jane Addams. Whether it is accurate or not to call it a resurgence, the ideas of many contemporary scholars derive from Dewey's educational doctrines. Dewey conceived of the educational process as democratic and liberal, related not to specific skills or strategies, but to the process of how people live socially in a democracy. In his view the purpose of education was to empower people, to help them acquire some measure of control over their own lives. According to Dewey, empowerment occurs through an experiential approach to learning, or, in the terms for which Dewey is best known, learning by doing.

Dewey's concern was with habits of thinking that cause us to place things and ideas into discontinuous classes or dualisms like those considered earlier in this text. "Learning" and "doing" or the "cognitive" and "affective" aspects of learning are dualities with which Dewey was particularly concerned. As he put it, we tend to think of emotions as purely private and personal. Except, perhaps, for the emotion of intellectual curiosity, feelings are thought to be distinct from the kind of pure intelligence that seeks to apprehend facts and truth. As he said, we consider "the intellect as a pure light; the emotions are a disturbing heat."

John Dewey's legacy is a philosophy of education that encourages the development of critical and creative thinking over traditional forms of rote and controlled learning. Experience is the core of his philosophy (Dewey, 1938). According to Dewey, experience involves principles of continuity and their organic interdependence and not the duality or distinctions of mankind and nature, mind and body, theory and practice, individual and society. In his view, learning is a process that takes place internally and subjectively. Dynamically active and ongoing, it is a process that constantly reconstructs and reorganizes experience by testing what is learned. As we find meaning in experience, our ability to direct the course of subsequent experiences, and to enhance growth and reflective thinking is increased (Dewey, 1916). Dewey was doubtful about learning based on the acquisition of knowledge from books and scholars. In this way his work anticipates Paulo Freire's objection to a banking system of learning in which knowledge is stored for future use in practice. Dewey referred to such an educational scheme as a "pedagogical fallacy," the erroneous assumption that previously acquired knowledge and theory will prepare the learner for the eventual demands of the real world. The best of theories, he said, will fall short of readying anyone to meet the incalculable contingencies of social life (Dewey, 1938). An even greater risk is that in our romance with the authority of theory we are likely to distrust our own reasoning, judgment, and imagination; we may allow theory to override our powerful intuitions.

Social work's key precept of "the person in the situation" corresponds with Dewey's premise that experience and learning are best understood in contextual terms. Social workers who are not programmed by this theory or that model are aware, not always comfortably, of the contextual ambiguities that intrude into our work with people in direct practice or social planning. At one moment, everything is in place; the next moment—with a subtle shift in the emotional climate, new information, a sudden recollection, the entry of another person, or the intrusion of other environmental factors—our certainty becomes tenuous. Our only recourse then is reflective inquiry and learning. This is what the reconstruction of experience is all about.

Overview of Experiential Learning

Let me insert a summary statement, a reiteration of the general principles of experiential learning. They will serve as a bridge or entry point into the literature of contemporary theorists on experiential learning, many of whom have elaborated on Dewey's ideas about the links that integrate learning and experience.

Learning is an ongoing subjective process that balances participation in the contextual world of experience with knowledge (facts, information, and practical skills). Learning in its full sense is equated with personal and social growth. At best, learning becomes part of the narratives of our existence, the life stories that symbolize our identities and guide how we cope with the ethical, interpersonal, and goal-directed demands of living. Learning is expressed in reflective thought and action, in confidence about one's wisdom tested by experience and shaped by a mind that is open to new and possibly contradictory knowledge. Simply put, learning is an active, intentional manifestation of consciousness.

The table on the following page, "Overview of the Elements of Experiential Learning," is a precise outline that, in its detail, would appear to sketch out an explanation of learning. Its purpose, however, is more functional. It is meant to serve as an aid or a guide for readers in making their way through the explication of the foundations and the stages, styles, and types of learning. Like the architecture of most outlines or theoretical structures we encounter, the table suggests logical order and progression. But learning, especially experiential learning, is rarely an orderly, incremental, sequential process. It may be guided by, but does not always conform to, such objective expectations as those spelled out in course outlines and curricula. The latter may define the specific objectives of teaching, but learning is an experience of another order. Learning involves the learner's curiosity, needs, intentions, and personal state of being. Still, learning is not entirely chaotic, especially when teachers take account of and respect the singularity of the learner. Teachers may then recognize a certain personal order and logic perhaps very unlike their own, yet as meaningful to the students as teachers' tendencies are to themselves.

There is another important point to make about the process of learning. Where some theoretical structures imply the beginning, development, and culmination of something, learning, as described here, has no firm beginning or final ending. To be sure, there are closed episodes of learning where the mastery of a par-

Overview of the Elements of Experiential Learning

Types of Intelligence
- Interpersonal
- Intrapersonal
- Linguistic
- Logical-Mathematical
- Spatial
- Bodily-Kinesthetic
- Musical

Conventional Teaching Modes
- Programmed Instruction
- Lecture and Discussion
- Problem-Centered/Case Study
- Experiential Learning Model: Stages
- Concrete Experience
- Reflective Observation
- Abstract Conceptualization
- Active Experimentation

Reflective Learning Process
- Pre-reflective
- Radical Relativism
- Reflective Thinking

Learning Styles
- Divergent
- Convergent
- Assimilative

Learning Contexts
- Affective
- Perceptual
- Cognitive
- Behavioral

Critical Analysis and Discourse
- Collegial Teaching-Learning Roles
- Teacher as student
- Student as teacher

ticular functional skill or method may have a start and conclusion. We might say that the student *begins* to learn social work (or any other subject) upon entry into the academic program, but that is only a temporal designation, a matter of record keeping.

As to the ending of learning, there is none apart from the rituals and credentials that honor the accomplishments measured by institutional standards and requirements. At best, educators should hope that students' relatively brief period of formal professional educational will be the springboard, the impetus, for a lifetime of learning. At worst, we should hope that the same period will not prove to be a deterrent.

Constraints and Opportunities

With the Overview as a guide, we now take a more exacting look at the foundations of experiential learning, to start with its constraints and opportunities. The discussion will begin with the work of Howard Gardner (1991), perhaps best known for his writing on multiple intelligences. This discussion, however, will concentrate on Gardner's *The Unschooled Mind* (1991), which deals with problems of schooling in general. Gardner's perspective on teaching and learning can be extrapolated to the constraints inherent in professional education. Gardner argues against what Dewey called the "pedagogical fallacy," the idea that knowledge gained in the classroom will be effective in grappling with the contingencies of real-life situations. Gardner, however, bases his argument on the findings of educational research collected over the past decades. This research reveals that educational programs that appear to be successful, that bring about expected outcomes, typically fail to achieve their most important mission (p. 3). Overt signs of classroom success like high test scores or positive evaluations by classroom teachers do not predict comparable success when students try to take on the diverse actualities of their professional practice.

Gardner uses the study of physics as a case in point, but also extends these findings to mathematics, the social sciences, and the humanities. He argues that even high-achieving honor students in college-level courses are frequently unable to solve basic problems and questions encountered in a form slightly different from those on which they have been formally instructed and tested. It is not that these learners just "draw a blank" or try to reconfigure what they learned. Rather, they ignore what they have been taught and blithely resort to the simplistic or stereotypical solutions that they previously banked on.

Gardner mentions the constraints that tend to perpetuate the classical or traditional form of education that were mentioned in the previous section on the roots of social work. They are, of course, not perceived as constraints but as the accepted customs of the culture of education, the way we have always done things. As customs, they need no defense and, in fact, are readily called on to defend the status quo when questions are raised or new ideas are introduced. For example, consider the limits and directions imposed by the history and epistemology of social work, the ideology and mission of the profession combined with the theories and persuasions of certain dominant personalities. When propositions that compete with these traditions are submitted, the reaction often is some sophisticated variation on the justification, "But this is how we always have done it." There are, in addition, the boundaries and limits created by the rules of academic institutions and the profession. Obviously, the structure, standards, and procedures of the educational institution will control how teaching and learning should occur. When, on occasion, educational scholars question whether the standard semester system or required classroom hours fit the goals of professional education, the response is some form of "You can't fight the system." It follows, then, that course structures, curricula, and objectives that conform to these strictures legitimize these constraints.

"Constraint" is not always a negative term. It can refer to human functions that are adaptive. Physiologically, certain muscles, for example, inhibit strain or injury to the body; certain blocking functions of the brain prevent overload. Innate constraints also serve students well in grappling with the sometimes overwhelming demands of learning. Constraints shape the personal characteristics, the singularity of learners, and are evident in the unique styles, world views, and objectives that predispose them to certain modes of learning. In other words, students are armed with idiosyncratic strengths and limits; call them "learning needs." They must sort through these to get what they can from any educational experience. Gardner's theory of "multiple intelligences" is useful in sharpening our appreciation of such individual differences and their implications for the process of becoming a social worker.

This theory, as Gardner (1993b) explains, diverges from the traditional operational understanding of intelligence as the ability to answer items on standardized (IQ) tests of intelligence. The results of such standardized tests are what psychologists call *g* (general intelligence) scores. Commonly, they are tests measuring basic verbal, mathematical, and spatial aptitudes and abilities. Multiple intelligence theory, on the other hand, pluralizes the traditional concept of intelligence. As I will indicate, there are several intelligences (or ways of understanding and dealing with the world), each consisting of a special ability to solve a particular problem or create a particular product. Each of these intelligences is predicated on one's innate biological attributes and takes form accordingly. Or to put it another way, intelligence in Gardner's view is not the distinct intellectual faculty measured by IQ scores, but an attribute that is continuous and interactive with emotion, biology, and culture. As Gardner notes, even a universal skill such as language may manifest itself particularly as writing in one culture, as oratory in another, and as a distinctive dialect in a third. Gardner (1983, 1993a, 1993b) describes the evolutionary and biological evidence suggesting the existence of seven kinds of intelligence. In what follows, I will outline his theory of seven intelligences to show their implications for the education of social workers.

Types of Intelligence

The first two intelligences are familiar and, for the most part, are requisite to social work education and practice: they are the *interpersonal* and *intrapersonal* intelligences (Gardner, 1993b). Interpersonal intelligence, also called social intelligence, is the core capacity to notice distinctions in others. In particular, this talent encompasses being sensitive to mood, temperaments, motivations, and intentions in relationships with others. It is an aptitude of religious leaders, teachers, and parents. Interpersonal intelligence involves not just a curiosity about the human condition but an empathic talent for engaging with others in an enabling manner. Some individuals possessing this talent are intrigued by the interactional complexities of groups; others are drawn to the mysteries of mind, brain, and behavior. Still others are interested in the role of culture, politics, and other forces in personal and community life. At its best, this talent, according to Arthur Koestler (1964), is the "moment of truth, the sudden emergence of a new insight, an act of intuition. Such intuitions give the appearance of miraculous flashes, or short-circuits of reasoning" (p. 211).

Intrapersonal intelligence, or a keen sense of self, tends to be an attribute that is accepted as a given in professional education for social work. This intelligence involves knowledge of one's range of emotions, the ability to discriminate among them, and the ability to guide one's behavior in social affairs. In a manner of speaking, intrapersonal intelligence is not as visible as other aptitudes and is more readily discerned in its interaction with the other intelligences. It often works in combination with interpersonal intelligence and with the linguistic abilities that make for excellence in oral and literary skills.

With *linguistic intelligence* we begin to address certain talents that, if they are attended to at all, may be seen as incidental or ancillary in relation to the basic requirements of professional education for social work. To be sure, all students are expected to be able to communicate coherently orally and in writing, if only to survive the academic demands of the educational experience. But for some individuals, linguistic skill is a special strength that deserves encouragement and cultivation. Individuals with linguistic talent are able to express their understanding with particular power.

Logical-mathematical intelligence can, in many cases, be equated with the scientific mind that readily dissects reality into its parts or variables. The individual possessing this talent can juggle a number of mental functions, transforming them into hypotheses that can be tested and evaluated. Mathematics might be the language of understanding used to create rational explanations of causal relations. Here, the learner may be drawn to forms of inquiry that are empirical and positivist in nature, searching to discover certain logical and linear structures.

Spatial intelligence, like the remaining three forms, may not at first glance seem to be as pertinent to social work education as the ones mentioned above. Yet, for many students and practitioners, spatial talents may be the source for creative learning and practice. With spatial intelligence, for example, one is likely to visualize the world from angles and aspects not available to ordinary perception. This kind of visualization is like that of the visual artist who is adroit in working with colors, shapes, forms, and perspective, revising reality into unique visions and images. Structural family therapy might be an appealing approach to learners and practitioners with this kind of intelligence insofar as it offers a canvas upon which the multi-forms of family interaction can be drawn, leading to some insights about how family members might be repositioned, both physically and psychologically. Art therapy would also utilize this talent insofar as the therapist may help clients visualize and thereby better express their understandings of self and circumstances.

A unique example of this intelligence in action is the work of Brennen Taylor and Ann Taylor (1993, 1997) who recognized that problems in spatial relations are often overlooked in the adaptations of certain clients, especially those who are mentally and physically challenged. Under the Taylors' rubric of "wayfinding," these are people who need assistance in dealing with travel, how to get from one location to another, especially when their destination is a provider of needed services. Directions alone may not suffice. These people need help in learning how to judge distances and recognize landmarks, as well as in selecting and boarding various means of public transportation.

Bodily-kinesthetic intelligence is evident in dancers and athletes most prominently. We also notice this intelligence in people whom we admire for their masterly ability to repair, build, or invent objects with exceptional motor skills. There are social work students and professionals who in some ways think with their bodies, are aware of certain rhythms, and need movement to express their thoughts and feelings. They may employ dance therapy directly, to enhance freedom of movement or the expression of body awareness, or they may simply be sensitive to the way the body and its posture can be more telling than words used.

Like other intellectual skills, whether mathematical or linguistic, *musical intelligence* uses its own language to symbolize our lives, the world, and experience. Musical therapists use melody to stir the imagination and enliven and free the mind. The social worker who has musical intelligence can use this sensitivity to achieve a deeper understanding of and closeness with clients. A good example is narrated in Mary Tasker's (1999) essay on working with adolescents taken with the allure of rap and hip-hop music. While the music was alien to her own lifestyle and musical tastes, Tasker invited these youngsters to introduce her to their music and teach her its meaning for them. Their newfound awareness deepened the young people's affinity in ways that ordinary words and deeds could not achieve.

These theories on the manifestations of intelligence can be considered as empirical metaphors to the extent that they actually represent the range of attributes and artistry we witness in the dispositions of people we know or of those we admire from afar. In agency settings or academe, we are often astounded by the colleague who, seemingly, from somewhere "out in left field" or "off the wall" or "out of the box" will propose a solution or idea so radical, so beyond our ken, as to invite ridicule or mirth—that is, unless we try to see the matter from within this peculiar frame of reference. For a time, some years ago, De Bono's (1973) book on lateral thinking encouraged appreciation of this talent.

For educators, awareness of such talents adds depth and meaning to the aphorism that we must respect individual differences. Educators who are open and receptive to the unique talents of their students can serve as models that will encourage learners to be equally receptive to the uncommon qualities, strengths, and abilities of their clients. Many of my students introduced new metaphors into my thinking on the knowledge and practice of social work. My musically talented students got me to think of the practitioner as an accompanist, one who provides the harmonic ambience against which the client can, as a soloist, try out new voices or performances. Those with linguistic intelligence depicted the social worker as an editor who helped clients "rewrite" the stories of their lives in more rewarding ways. And, of course, my students who were endowed with logical-mathematical skills frequently kept me on course by questioning my sometimes metaphysical flights.

It is worth noting again that education for experiential learning has a greater purpose than educating the learner. Ultimately, it has implications for the client's growth and change. When students are consciously awakened to the worth of their own capabilities, talents, and potential in the process of learning through experience, they might appreciate that their clients are equally able to grow in the same manner. In this view, education for professional practice would not be regarded as an esoteric or privileged event that one undergoes *in order* to become a social worker. Instead it would be seen as an approach to living and understanding that is equally applicable to clients' ability to realize their prospects for coping with their problems of living.

There are other insights to be garnered by a keener awareness of individual differences, since such distinctive world views often shape an individual's distinguishing life theme. We may better understand the values and predispositions that, in the first place, prompt a person to choose social work as a career. Consider also that these diverse perceptions might also account for the sharp and sometimes caustic debates that divide educators. The debates that persist about the shape of the curriculum, what students ought to know, the nature of "effectiveness" in its many realms, or what outcomes are preferable are not always power struggles. Sometimes they reflect sincere and credible differences in how the "real world" ought to be defined.

Specifically, the question of which modes of inquiry are "best" becomes moot if we take account of individual differences. Certainly, the precise nature of the research question may have some bearing on which research modality should be employed. At the same time, the particular world view of the researcher will also manifest itself in the design of the project. Those whose talents reside in the domain of logical-mathematical reasoning will have much to offer on the values and limits of empirical and quantitative methods; others, whose leanings are more interpersonal and linguistic, could be instructive about the use of ethnographic or other qualitative approaches. In the final analysis, we need to discard the "one method fits all" system of teaching social work research and encourage students to seek their own modes of inquiry, to find the best mode for making sense of the question that teases them.

To make this point, and to underscore the power of particular, if not peculiar, intelligences as they bear on how we investigate inner worlds or outer space, Gardner (1993a) compares the idiosyncratic pursuits of Sigmund Freud and Albert Einstein. In some ways, the two major figures seem to be similar, for instance, in coming from upwardly mobile Jewish homes in Germany in the same era. But from an early age, Freud's interests were directed toward other human beings, whereas Einstein's centered on the world of objects and the forces of nature. As Gardner sums up, it is unlikely that either man, as a normal scientist, could have come up with the other's discoveries. They had different kinds of minds and operated with different kinds of symbols. Freud was strong in the linguistic and personal intelligences: a shrewd observer of human nature, he thought primarily in terms of language with hardly any spatial or logical content. In sharp contrast, Gardner says, Einstein's linguistic skills and interests in the personal sphere were strictly limited. As a physical scientist, his thoughts were rich with visual-spatial images that could be related to experiments and mathematical formalisms that existed within a tight logical-mathematic structure. Freud and Einstein shared a scientific personality and, as scientific revolutionaries, were ambitious, dogged, and willing to stand alone with their respective ideas. But their scientific endeavors could not be more different.

Implications of Intelligence Theory on Experiential Education

The implications of the theory of multiple intelligences carry us into what Gardner (1991) calls the *apprenticeship* model of education—a combination of experiential and mentorship teaching and learning. Tracing the long history of apprenticeship, he guesses that the reason for the decline of this mode of learning is that it may seem old-fashioned, associated with the mastery skills and crafts that have largely disappeared in the industrial age. Gardner notes that even in the professions, where apprenticeship would still seem highly appropriate, it has been replaced by lengthy scholastic regimes that culminate in credentialing or certification. The credentialing is thought to constitute an end in itself and appears to furnish the quality control that is difficult to provide in an apprenticeship. Consider the amount of "objective" data—grades, frequency of class participation, attendance, scores achieved on required written assignments—used in the decision to grant a bachelor's or master's degree or a license for professional practice. Still, whatever they measure about "knowing," they cannot tell us much about performance.

If performance or the capability to work helpfully with clients or fulfill other professional responsibilities is a valid measure, then the apprenticeship model mentioned by Gardner should be highly valued. Field instructors can attest to the heavily contextualized nature of the practicum and the opportunities it offers for appraising the progress and potential of the individual learner. There are milestones that can be used to gauge the learner's professional growth in practice, collegiality, ethical responsibility, and knowledge. The setting itself provides rich opportunities for learning. When there is a task at hand, relevant knowledge can be sought and applied at the precise moment it is needed. Simply put, the apprenticeship model, or experiential learning, offers these occasional learning moments when everything comes together in a meaningful way, when "knowing" becomes internalized, owned. At this point, theory is no longer a purely intellectual axiom nor is a skill or act purely behavioral.

The issue of multiple intelligences also has some interesting implications for the admission of students into social work programs. Typically, programs employ a variety of measures or standards as selection criteria—for example, prior academic achievement, the ability to communicate effectively, and applicants' clarity about their educational and professional objectives. As indicators, these standards test only the narrow range of intellectual skills that are relevant to a traditional educational model. Thus, these standards may very well predict academic success, especially since the next advanced stages in education the student is pursuing will be fairly consistent with the philosophy of education of prior programs, even though the content will be different (Pelech, Stalker, Regehr, & Jacobs, 1999). Simply put, successful academic performance on one level of education fairly well predicts success on the next. But such academic standards cannot always predict one's success in the *performance* of social work. Not only are we unsure what such "success" would look like, but as I want to show, the linguistic and logical-mathematical abilities that are valued by the academy are not necessarily the only or even the major forms of intelligence required for becoming a competent professional social worker.

An educational program that relies on narrow standards and expectations will likely not encourage the opportunities for learning that can be capacious, liberal, and opportune. And again, such standards may not address or credit the variety of talents (or intelligences) that students bring to their education. Since individuals differ in the strengths of certain intelligences, these differences will complicate the process of human learning and understanding (Gardner, 1991). Without serendipitous good fortune or the sensitive perception of an educator these talents may not be recognized or maximized.

The principle of individual differences or diversity in the learning process urges us to look more closely at the nature of experiential learning and the many ways it addresses and builds on the variations in talent and style among learners. After all, excellence in teaching is the keen ability to recognize and augment these singular variations, the ability to enable students to discover their respective strengths as learners. Education that pays little heed to these individual differences becomes a blunt instrument.

Experiential learning is strongly related to theories of adult learning, or andragogy, insofar as it is based on the adult learner's needs and objectives. Direct experience provides the opportunity for learners to analyze their endeavors and their application to their career and life situations (Sims & Sims, 1995, p. 3-5). Among the many adult learning theorists, Malcolm Knowles's (1984) assumptions make this connection clear, since they apply directly to preparations for professional careers.

Adults, first of all, are motivated to learn by their individual goals in life; thus, the learner's needs and interests are the appropriate starting points for organizing educational activities. Adult orientation to learning is life- or work-centered; therefore the appropriate frameworks for education need to be life- or work-related situations. It follows that opportunities for self-directed participation, analysis, and application constitute the richest resources for learning. Adult education gives special attention to individual differences in life experience, personal style, time, place, and pace of learning. In contrast to traditional education where knowledge is accrued for its own sake or for future purposes, in experiential education the immediacy of the problem or task at hand is the major impetus of adult learning.

Responsibility for learning falls to the individual learner with the teacher or mentor providing the resources and creating the climate and inspiration for learning. The teacher can also serve as a model for the learner.

Teaching Modes

To gain some perspective, let me first locate experiential learning within the general array of teaching modes that, in progression, offer students increasing opportunities to explore how they apply knowledge to real world conditions and problems (Sims & Sims, 1995). I will then show how these teaching modes apply to social work education. We start with programmed instruction, the least concerned with student-centered learning. We then proceed in order of increasing emphasis on student-centered learning to lecture and discussion, problem-centered learning, experiential learning, and critical analysis.

Programmed instruction transmits systematic information and allows for lower-level skill learning. An example from social work education might be an introductory class in statistical research or computer language. *Lecture and discussion* is designed to transfer large amounts of information in some depth. Students may gain a certain knowledge base but usually without the direct opportunity to apply this knowledge to actual circumstances. Examples here might include courses on human behavior and social welfare policy. *Problem-centered learning* can occur in classrooms or seminars where the students heuristically apply concepts and theories to real-world situations. The case-study approach is the cornerstone of this mode, and it is most evident in courses on social work practice and research.

Programmed instruction, lecture and discussion, and problem-centered learning represent the normative modes of teaching of academe. They need not be mutually exclusive. Any course may employ any and all of the three modes, depending on the learning objectives. In addition, the "articulated approach" to social work education described earlier may link these teaching modes with field experience to establish a working relationship between cognitive and experiential learning. Although the next two modes, *experiential learning* and *critical analysis*, are more easily adapted to the practicum, they can be applied in the academic classroom as well. And, as we will later consider, they might be even more richly exploited if class and field were unified in some way.

Kolb's (1984) experiential learning model (ELM) is useful as a framework for outlining the stages in which the process and individual styles of learning can affect learning. Although the four stages of this model—*concrete experience, reflective observation, abstract conceptualization*, and *active experimentation*—are presented in their logical sequence, in real-life, learning can be initiated at any stage. Thus, although the stages of learning may be planned out by the teacher (or collegially) to cover a particular period of time, any stage of learning can precede any other. The sudden emergence of a particular problem or question that requires abstract conceptualization means only that problems requiring reflective observation will come later. Given that social work practice is embroidered with the many complexities of human circumstance, even the simplest case will pose dilemmas for which students cannot be prepared in advance.

Learning Stages

Concrete Experience. In Kolb's model learning begins with a concrete experience, a real-life event or problem that illuminates concepts, principles, or generalizations. An instructor might ask students to analyze an observed interview, a role-play, or a section of an agency's regulations, or the concrete experience could arise out of students' curiosity and questions. In either case, the experience itself is used to engender inductive, or bottom-up, learning about a specific issue in conceptual and operational terms. Simply put, learning begins with these fundamental questions: What is going on? What does it mean? What do I need to know to make sense of it?

Reflective Observation. Within the reflective observation stage, these questions guide the ongoing process of learning. For a good example of this stage, I return to the mentorship of Mr. Milner. At one point in my fumbling practice with a certain client in my field agency, I was baffled by what struck me as peculiar in my client's reactions to my good intentions. My hesitation about revealing my incompetence to Mr. Milner was overpowered by my desperation. He listened with care and sympathy, nodded, and said, "It's just transference." I wasn't very sure what the term meant, but it was reassuring to know at that moment that this puzzling behavior had a name or belonged to some classification. It is a basic human need to be able to classify reality and experience. If you know what something is, you believe you are better able to deal with it. The reordering and reconceptualizion of reality that is expected in this stage of reflective observation can unfold in many ways beyond the mere presentation of deductive information. Readings can be assigned, the question can be a topic for group discussion, and students can be asked to relate the event in question to other life experiences.

This stage also offers the opportunity for both the teacher and student to gain at least a hint of the kind of intelligence the student tends to fall back on when beginning to think about and reflect on concrete experience. For example, when asked to comment on the physical layout of an agency's waiting room and reception area, the intrapersonally oriented student might reflect on how it might feel to be a client in that room. The student with interpersonal leanings might wonder about the question of privacy, or how waiting clients might deal with each other. The musically talented student might suggest that the austerity of the setting be softened by piped-in melodies.

Abstract Conceptualization. This stage advances reflective observation to a point where the learner begins, in a manner of speaking, to "own" knowledge. In other words, concepts or theories grasped by the intellect alone, in this stage, are integrated into the mind of the learner. They are not imprinted like Xerox copies but are given their special form by the individual's cognitive style, talents or intelligence, life experiences, and world view. More than just stored data, this new knowledge joins with intuitions arising out of other life experiences. Thoughts about how the new knowledge might creatively be applied mingle with emerging hypotheses about how things and behavior work, as well as other conscious and subjective understandings.

The satisfactions of enlightenment are temporary, however, for new knowledge only reveals the limits of what one knows and not what still needs knowing. Returning to my "transference" example, my relief at knowing what to call my problem was short lived. I began to wonder about the meaning and validity of the term transference as an explanation of the human event in question. Although it felt almost heretical to doubt one of the authoritative canons of the healing arts (and my teacher as well), something about the concept of transference didn't quite fit the situation I was trying to understand. From my perspective, there were more pressing things at work than something hidden in the deep recesses of my client's early life. I felt compelled by my disquiet to consider other explanations and theories of learning and behavior more in accord with my predilections.

Active Experimentation. Obviously, the learning patterns that count, those that evolve into professional behavior, are more readily apparent in the face-to-face conditions of the practicum than in theory. This is especially the case in this, the fourth stage of the *Experiential Learning Model*, the active experimentation stage. Whether in role-play or in actual supervised practice, the learner is required to synthesize and apply what has been learned. In short, learning should be of a whole. If it is not, then specific problems will emerge in, for instance, how the student observes a problem or event, conceptualizes it, and reflectively integrates knowledge and experience. These problems should be visibly apparent. These are "learning moments" when, working together as colleagues, the mentor and student (or student group) can conjointly define the learning problem. For example, the field teacher might help the learner "see" certain exchanges that went unnoticed within the complexities of group dynamics, such as a member who subtly tends to change the subject when the discussion becomes intense. The student can then be helped to understand this pattern in conceptual terms and can proceed to reflect on its possible meanings as far as disabling the communication patterns of the group. Theory, reflection, and practice become integrated in such an experiential episode.

Reflective Learning Process

Learning that is more than just the acquisition and storage of information, learning that is open to reflection and inquiry, energizes a remarkable human attribute. It is the ability to think about what one is thinking, to doubt what one knows, to question conventional and therefore comforting wisdom, and most of all, to balance what one knows and believes against real world experience. This kind of thinking opens new corridors of exploration down which one goes in search of the sources and implications of an idea, a theory, or a method. When one is unwilling to make this journey, a closed, solipsistic mind that precludes the possibility of creative and responsive practice is the result.

Kitchener and King's (1981) extensive studies of students' learning patterns underscore the critical importance of this challenge to the learner's pre-existing network of assumptions. In effect, they caution educators not to assume that all students share the same abilities to engage in critical thinking, problem solving, reasoned judgment, and reflective thinking. Experience tells us that relatively few of our students enjoy such abilities, and therefore that the course of education often needs to shift from content to process. The focus on *what* needs to be known needs to shift to help students learn *how* to think about knowledge. As I will consider in the forthcoming discussion of critical discourse, the question of *how* to think about knowledge is particularly important in relation to the moral, ethical, and ideological questions that arise in practice.

Kitchener and King (1981) offer some helpful counsel with regard to identifying the nature and quality of learners' reasoning and reflection. Based on their research, they describe a seven-stage sequence of learning patterns, starting with somewhat primitive pre-reflective assumptions about knowledge and finishing with what they call mature reflective judgment. Each stage is characterized by a related set of assumptions or a frame of reference that the learner imposes on knowledge and reality, thereby influencing a particular pattern of learning. I will collapse the seven stages into the three that are most useful in sorting out some common problems in teaching and learning.

Pre-reflective. Students who function at the primary level or pre-reflective stage of learning are those who are sure there are some absolute answers "out there" and all that they have to do is locate the authority, human or textual, that will provide them with the "right" answers. Whatever reflective tendencies they have are circular, in a way. Students search for the selected facts, recipes, and rules that will prove what they thought they needed to know in the first place. This kind of learner really wants to know only "what works" with little tolerance for ambiguity or doubt. Unchallenged, he or she would drift toward and settle for a packaged mode of practice, or would be enticed by beguiling but passing fads or schools of practice.

Radical Relativism. The second stage is a radical version of the first, a move from absolutism to skepticism (if not cynicism) in how one regards the world of knowledge. The second stage student may indeed have reflected on the nature of knowledge, but she has come to the conclusion that there are literally no right answers, that nothing can *really* be known. Thus the student feels justified in believing in the kind of radical relativism that decrees any knowledge is as good as another, and the best one can do is what one thinks is right. In professional practice, the label "eclectic," "intuitive," or "by-the-seat-of-the-pants" practice may overly dignify this approach.

Reflective Thinking. The third stage represents the achievement of useful and mature reflective thought and judgment. Although one would expect that time and experience are necessary to arrive at this stage, with mentorship and collegiality in the teaching-learning experience, the practicum might produce the beginning signs of this growth. Optimally, the learner begins to find a degree of confidence that allows her to relinquish the belief that there are indeed ultimate truths and objective realities.

Unlike the radical relativist, however, she has not entirely abandoned the pursuit of knowledge and understanding. With a measure of curiosity and critical thinking she is aware that personal constructs about the world are, to some extent, reflective of time, social context, and history. At the same time, this reflective practitioner is confident about plausible and personally tested theories and constructs and is guided in practice by them. But as a life-long learner, she also knows that this knowledge must remain open to the new information that experience offers. To put it simply, this is the stage, or ideal that one reaches when one learns enough to realize how much more one needs yet to learn. It is this individual who is somewhat comfortable with ambiguity and thus open to the enigmas and obscurities of work involving individuals, families, groups, organizations, or communities.

As a means of helping social work students develop mature reflective thought and judgment, I'd like to introduce process recording. While it is not a new educational tool, over the years and for whatever reasons, process recording has fallen into disuse. When it is used, it tends to read like the literal minutes of a meeting. Process recording is typically a written follow-up to a practice event (e.g., interview, group meeting, community conference). Far more than a purely descriptive account, process recording does just that, records process. It requires the student to reflectively capture the essential content, flow, transactional nature, and meaning of a practice event. It attempts to track the helping experience, reconsidering past episodes and, in light of them, projecting future efforts.

Field instructors have recognized the value of process recording since the 1920s. This suggests that, in some ways, bygone educators had an intuitive grasp of the experiential ways in which one learns to become a social worker. In any event, Graybeal and Ruff (1995), noting the dearth of literature about or interest in process recording, make a case for this useful educational medium in the current educational scheme. For one thing, process recording complements the principles of adult learning. Instructors' feedback on student attempts to articulate an understanding of their work with clients will enable students to discover their preferred, even unique, learning and working styles. Second, process recording addresses the problems and objectives of learning noted above. As mentor and learner together carefully analyze the written record of a practice event, the particular stage of experiential learning where a student might be stuck should become immediately apparent. Altogether, Graybeal and Ruff agree that process recording is one of the best teaching methods for developing reflective thinking and practice.

Process recording and other dialogical methods of teaching and learning underscore the importance of the practicum as a focal point for professional education. The classroom is a comfortable climate for learning, an environment where students can, in an orderly way and at their own pace, explore singular frameworks, concepts, and methods. The field, in contrast, plunges the student into the disorder that characterizes the human condition. Not only must he respond to the uniqueness of each client's circumstances, he also needs to be attentive to the many exigencies that can impinge on practice. He must be mindful of such peripheral influences as the agency's ideologies as well as how the reactions of family members and the community, for example, may influence the process of helping. Given that the dilemma involves people and their relationships, there are always ethical quandaries and often uncertain compromises that the student must wade through. And there are no certainties about how anything will work out in the end.

Contingency is what makes experiential learning a very busy milling machine: cutting, shaping, and finishing the original raw product, refining a student's skills and knowledge to fit the requirements of real-life human situations. To complicate things further, experience is capricious; change begets change and, inevitably, the learning cycle restarts. Put another way, students should not be compliant beneficiaries of endowed knowledge. Rather, they should be proactive, engaged (by choice or expectation) in learning about how they learn, learning about what is unique and shared in their styles and perspectives as the foundation for a lifetime of learning. A well-structured field setting that utilizes the principles of experiential learning is one that will, by definition, be cognizant of how the contingencies of practice are keen opportunities for student growth and the nurturing of student confidence.

Learning Styles

As I have shown, personal attributes, along with attitudes that reflect the influences of culture and ethnicity, will intersect with students' preferences for certain modes of learning. These preferences, expressed in thought and action, are called *learning styles* (Rainey & Kolb, 1995). In the sense that these styles characterize the individual, they might be seen as the art or the leavening agent of effective learning and practice. As Schön (1987) observes:

> The student cannot be *taught* what he needs to know, but he can be *coached*. He has to *see* on his own behalf and in his own way the relations between means and methods employed and methods achieved. Nobody else can see for him, and he can't see just by being 'told,' although the right kind of telling may guide his seeing and thus help him see what he needs to see. (p. 17, emphasis added)

When teachers and mentors are attuned to the special learning styles of students, they are meeting the goals of diversity education in accord with the highest principles of democratic learning. Valuing and respecting a pattern of scholarship is not an easy task, especially when such patterns are at variance with one's own styles or with standard models of teaching and learning.

The importance of individual learning styles may be less apparent in the closed classroom, which offers students many covers and corners for escape. A student can get by in many instances by merely responding to a roll call, if that is the practice, or by offering a well-timed question or commentary. Just recently, my bright, thirteen-year-old grandson demurely told me how he has learned to ask his teachers the "right" questions, that is, those that will keep the teacher happy and talking for a while. He is well-prepared for the years of education ahead of him. In the field setting, such adaptive ploys would be easily spotted. Students are *there,* fully and completely, and their performance is observable within the bustle, stir, and pressures of the placement milieu. The open and aboveboard nature of the practicum will intensify the friction of unfamiliar differences in learning styles and, therefore, lead to the possibilities for dialogue that might ease the discord. The enlightenment that springs from colloquy between and among students and mentors offers several educational benefits (Sims & Sims, 1995).

First, it may be very important news to the student that she has something called an "individualized learning style." Not only does this new knowledge add to the student's identity or sense of self, but it alerts her to the value of others' learning styles. As we will see in the examples of programs using the experiential approach, an enormous amount of shared learning occurs when students join in groups to exchange their various approaches to problem solving. Together, these benefits expand students' awareness that how they think, learn, and act are not random activities, but are reflective of how they typically understand and cope with reality. This growing awareness will enable them to identify other learning needs and opportunities. They will be better able to seek and take help as needed, to accept constructive criticism, and to compare their way of learning with other active learning styles. Such self-knowledge can spark an ongoing process of evaluating one's effectiveness in a range of practice situations. And we should not overlook the implications of self-knowledge for practice. It hardly needs to be said that the more that one understands the motifs of one's own mind and behavior, the better able one is to understand how others think and act. Thus, as students become more cognizant of the idea that learning can take a variety of forms and styles, they are likely to be more appreciative of the diverse ways their clients make sense of experience and the exceptional ways in which they learn how to master the challenges that confront them.

To this point, I have discussed learning styles in general terms, largely to emphasize the importance of their function in the processes of learning. As personal styles, they are both various and often overlapping, recognized more as observable patterns than as definitive categories. With growing familiarity teachers come to "know" or intuitively grasp how this student, in contrast to that one, will deal with a particular problem. Still, it is useful to consider three kinds of learner, the *diverger*, the *converger*, and the *assimilator*, found in Rainey and Kolb's (1995) brief catalog and in Goldstein (1981b). These three learning styles represent the patterns of many social work students. In the discussion that follows I will use as examples composite figures of my former social work students.

As a *diverger*, Karla's thinking, her way of grasping reality, typically moved from the specific to the general. When the class discussed principles of diagnosis or assessment, for example, she would question the principles because she believed that there were just too many exceptions, that human behavior was just too complex and deep to be sorted into such neat categories. As evidence for her view she would refer to people she knew who had suffered the indignities of a label, and point out famous people whose notorious lives resisted neat classifications. Karla enjoyed brainstorming, often finding connections among ideas or events that puzzled more ordinary thinkers. Always ready to offer her slant on a situation, she was at the same time sensitive to other students' dilemmas. In her mind there were always other possibilities, other options. Paradoxically, despite her aversion to labels, when I commented on her learning style, she grinned, delighted with the understanding of why she seemed to irritate people when she wouldn't settle for what they were sure were obvious explanations. In practice she was most skillful in helping certain clients discover creative alternatives to their troubling circumstances.

As a *convergent* thinker, Alden's reasoning moved in the other direction, from the general to the specific. He would listen to a lecture or discussion with stern patience. Usually sooner than later, he would seek to refocus the discussion, wanting to come to a point. If he couldn't get the right answers, at least he wanted the right questions to direct his exploration. He was comfortable with theories, frameworks, and methods that, to him, served rational and practical functions. He often demanded that we stick to the course outline. Alden was particularly adept at problem solving and decision making if he was allowed to sort the facts that could be lined up in cause-effect terms. In this way, he was especially helpful to clients who needed to find order in their world and get their lives on track.

Della's style as an *assimilato*r was more ambiguous than the styles of the other two students. Hers was at times a blend of the former two styles of learning. She had considerable aptitude for thinking about models and theories that structured knowledge in explicit terms. She was drawn to the systematic method and protocols of empirical research and found some rewards in working out hypotheses and isolating essential variables. She was also partial to the kind of rigorous thinking necessary for social planning and policy development. She looked for the "big picture" or the well-organized structure. Her term papers were well organized, blocked out in advance of writing the first word. In practice, she enjoyed working with community projects and with administrative planning.

These learning styles reflect certain dispositions to learning; most people are, to some degree, able to resort to the style of learning appropriate to the task they face. For example, Karla, the diverger, disliked the restrictions of some multiple-choice tests, yet would discipline herself to respond as required. And in an emergency, even Alden would use as much imagination as he could to discover new styles and solutions. Although current learning theorists do not make the connection, we need to consider how individual learning styles are linked to, or are functions of, the individual's talents or intelligences. We might assume that Della's learning style is probably related to her spatial and linguistic talents; Alden's skills lie perhaps in the realm of the logical-mathematical; and Karla seems guided by her intra- and interpersonal talents and linguistic skills.

There is persuasive evidence that heightened awareness of learning styles makes field instruction more rewarding and productive for both students and field instructors (Raschick, Maypole, & Day, 1998). Raschick, Maypole and Day applied Kolb's learning style model to a field education program involving 45 students and 40 field supervisors. Improvements were found in students' satisfaction with their field education and in student–field supervisor relationships. Of greater importance, the authors were surprised by the positive changes that occurred when both teachers and students came to recognize and appreciate the influence of their respective learning styles. Both groups began to frame their discussions of learning and practice in terms of their individual learning styles, thereby taking increasing responsibility for their learning needs and patterns and the implications of their style for practice.

The Contexts of Learning

I have concentrated on the characteristics of the learner, the traits, talents, and tendencies that identify individual learning needs. It is important to keep in mind that learning, like most human behaviors, is context-dependent. In other words, how and what one learns is influenced by the time and place of the experience and the opportunities it provides. Just as social work gives careful attention to the "person in the situation," learners in their educational settings also deserve careful study. Traditional settings, like the lecture halls, classrooms, or seminar rooms that make up the university's educational environment, are relatively uniform and consistent. Obviously, this is not the case when it comes to the practicum. There the setting can be anything from a one-person outpost to a well-staffed department in a host institution. The practicum setting may offer intimate, interpersonal services or may represent a veritable social service shopping mall. Field placements are situated in diverse locales that include hospitals, schools, housing projects, or mental health clinics.

Such settings, despite their differences, are selected to provide one common thing, the opportunity for active learning about how to become a social worker. Therefore, it is important to determine the common educational denominator within the mix of settings that allows for this learning to occur. To put this another way, irrespective of the structural and functional differences among field settings, each setting must offer a similar range of opportunities for learning—the basic knowledge, values, and skills required to become a competent social worker. At the helm of the practicum is, of course, the field faculty who will provide the necessary educational guidance.

There are many ways of defining what these field learning opportunities should look like. Some educators will contend that the practicum should focus on the content of learning. Others will emphasize process or the attainment of specific methodological objectives. Consistent with the theories that apply to adult learning, I want to stay with the postulate that *how,* or in what manner people learn, should take precedence over *what* they learn. The grasp of content, the understanding of process, and the attainment of specific behavioral and intellectual objectives, whether they are interviewing or assessment skills, will naturally follow. Sometimes primarily in one or another form, but more often in some combination or sequence, learning occurs *affectively*, *perceptually*, *cognitively*, and *behaviorally* (Rainey & Kolb 1995). This means, then, that just as every field setting should be responsive to students' learning styles and other personal attributes, it must also provide a learning context suited to their modes of learning.

The immense variability of the agencies and organizations in which schools of social work place students brings to mind the benefits of having a generalist orientation to social work practice. From such a perspective, one can pinpoint occasions and prospects for a common base for contextual learning. Whether the practicum is located in a large, busy institution like a hospital, public welfare office, public housing development, or a small outpost or crisis center, the mind of the generalist always is alert to the general principles and values of social work in the specific activities of planning, practice, and service delivery. Certainly, the acuity and imagination of the individual field teacher may generate other opportunities. The outline of and commentary on the four aspects of contextual learning just mentioned will clarify these assumptions.

Affectively oriented learning. Learning that occurs in this scenario complements the concrete experience stage. Here, the learner's attitudes, feelings, and values generated in here-and-now experiences are what count. At this stage, the learner is invited to stand back and take a fresh, first-hand look at the particular setting, its components, and routines. The teacher, as a role model and colleague, introduces an energizing climate of openness and feedback where students are invited not only to express their sentiments, but also to defend them in responsibly critical and reflective ways. Not unexpectedly, students are likely to judge the placement in relation to their expectations and personal goals, their notion of what service delivery should be like, or what they hoped to learn. As new experiences arise, they may voice their dismay or surprise about certain routines of service delivery. Far more than just the ventilation of feelings or gripe sessions, in these exchanges students are helped to understand (in Dewey's terms) that the affective, cognitive, and performance dimensions of learning are not separable; they shape the gestalt of the significant learning experience.

Perceptually oriented learning. As students begin to learn how to both trust *and* question their feelings and intuitions in response to a particular client's situation, they might say that "it feels right" to do this or that, or that one approach " just works better" than another, or that their values tell them it would be more ethical if the agency pursued one path instead of another. The role of the mentor is to encourage learners to translate these sentient impressions or generalizations into reasonable conjectures. This is not an abstract, intellectual experience floating above reality, but a situation-based process that has to make usable sense out of a concrete event—a real-life experience in practice with people. In this context, reflective learning is set in motion when personal values are put to the test, assumptions are questioned, and students surrender to their manner of defining reality. Simply put, progressive thought and reflection begin to augment the learner's native, perhaps intuitive talents and learning styles. In the deepest sense, from a bottom-up pathway learners begin know how their beliefs stand up when they are tested *in relation to* circumstantial events.

Cognitively oriented learning. Throughout the process of organizing their beliefs and knowledge, students can be helped to see the functional relationships between observed events and the conceptual themes, theories, or ideologies that purport to explain them. Here we see reflective integration at work as students explore how things work in real life from a variety of theoretical perspectives.

Let us say that students are exposed to the theory of social constructionism. In their minds, such theories are high-level abstractions about the roles of language and the influence of culture in the way people construct their version of reality. That is, of course, good to know—perhaps for some students an exciting idea. But the theory does not really jell as a working concept until its meaning emerges in the give and take of real-life communication. Malekoff, in *Group Work with Adolescents* (1997), gives us a useful example. A youngster speaks up about school administrators in a special high school group composed of immigrant

Latino youth. He complains, "They really don't care. . . they never listen to us. . . they think that just because we are different, we are garbage, right?" (p. 203). Now this might be regarded as fairly typical teenage talk, an "It's them, not us" protest. But was this the case? With the concept of social constructionism the group leader might come to a different conclusion. From a social constructivist perspective these youths might be understood as saying that something very critical was missing in their treatment by the high school administration. In the students' view, it was *personalismo,* a sensitive way of relating to people as people, not as subjects or members of a class or as "garbage." In sum, cognitive understanding kicks in when, in learners' minds, a mutual transfer occurs, when the raw experience in practice is transformed into something meaningful by the application of a theory.

The behaviorally oriented learning context. This category, created by educational theorists, is almost redundant. In the contexts of learning just sketched, the student is by no means an inert, passive recipient of knowledge. Either vicariously or actively, the learner is involved and animatedly engaged in learning. Consonant with the active experimentation stage of Kitchener and King's (1981) model of reflective learning, the behaviorally oriented learning context is a point where the various pieces of learning come together and, optimally, blend into a graceful and confident management of the helping experience. Management doesn't mean control. Rather, it suggests poise and confidence in the learner's use of professional wisdom and sensitivity to address the complexity of human encounters.

At this stage the learner is not mindlessly driven by theory, or navigating by method. Instead, he or she is mindfully and reflectively aware and, at best creatively able, to grasp the human/social situation in many metaphorical ways (Langer, 1997). In place of the sober term "dysfunctional," a very troubled family might be described as a "den of angry lions." Another example of the creative use of metaphor is found in Marsiglia's (1991) work with and study of a group of young Puerto Rican men. This was a diverse group of high school students similar to the group Malekoff describes. But Marsiglia found a way of giving the boys their special identity by the creative use of metaphor. Although all of the group's members were Puerto Rican, each naturally tended to define himself with certain cultural nuances. Marsiglia, as the group leader, suggested to them that group members who had recently immigrated and spoke only Spanish were the *poets*. The *warriors* were bilingual; they spoke in an African-American idiom and because they aggressively protected the poets, they were often suspended from school. The *traders* were very practical, able to navigate both worlds and cultures. And the *lawyers* looked Caucasian, spoke standard English, and were preppy in dress. They got along with and defended the warriors, but cautiously avoided trouble.

The ability to think and practice in metaphoric terms reflects the kind of confidence that supplants insecurity and self-consciousness. It indicates that the learner is receptive to the aesthetics of the helping experience and capable of looking beyond bleak psychological labels to grasp the wonder of the human mind, the strengths that, despite adversity, strive to find harmony. One of the implications of mastery in this context of learning is that it marks the beginning of professional accountability. For it is within the actual professional encounter, the "doing" of social work, that being, believing, knowing, talent, and ability converge.

Experiential Learning as Foundation for Critical Analysis and Discourse

Students who achieve the integrated goals of learning described thus far would be prepared to serve as professionals in effective ways. What I mean by "effective" is the ability to work with a measure of mature autonomy while, at the same time, knowing that learning is never finished but is always in process. For the reflective social worker, practice becomes the experiential medium for the unceasing and ever deepening search for understanding and meaning and for the maturation of one's personal helping style.

Becoming the effective social worker just defined, is, of course, the desired outcome of professional education. But I believe that room and opportunities need to be made for our students to pursue still higher standards of learning and performance. I speak here about the ability to engage in critical analysis and discourse.

Critical analysis and discourse are needed to advance the social work objectives of fostering and furthering social well-being. Social workers also need leadership in strengthening the role of our profession in society. Although such ideals may not be overlooked in conventional educational methods, their realization will be more likely when students are given the opportunity to engage in critical thought, analysis, and discourse. Progress in such learning is most often actualized within collegial dialogue among teachers and students.

Let me start with the commendable premises of the Council on Social Work Education Curriculum Policy Statement (CPS) (1992) as the groundwork for my proposals. The first part of the CPS, titled "Premises Underlying Social Work Education" (M3.0), emphasizes education that promotes "the development and advancement of knowledge, practice skills, and services." This objective would, generally speaking, fit the stages of experiential learning considered thus far. But there is an additional set of objectives that propose that learners should be prepared to "alleviate poverty, oppression, and discrimination" and to "further the well-being of people and promote social and economic justice." As an addendum to the otherwise educationally focused content of the CPS, this group of august objectives is, or should be, an extension of the profession's Code of Ethics (National Association of Social Workers, 1996). For as Isaiah Berlin (1990) advises,

> Such ideas are the substance of ethics. Ethical thought consists of the systematic examination of the relations of human beings to each other, the conceptions, interests, and ideals from which human ways of treating one another spring, and the systems of value on which such ends of life are based. These beliefs about how life should be lived, what men and women should be and do, are objects of moral inquiry, and when applied to groups and nations, and, indeed, mankind as a whole, are called political philosophy, which is but ethics applied to a society. (p. 1–2)

Although there may be an implied link between the first statement on "the development of knowledge" and the second statement on "the alleviation of poverty" what is missing is any definitive suggestion about the nature of the professional knowledge, leverage, and skill required to deal with or even think about ethical and moral problems of such magnitude and complexity. For example, do these statements call for the ability to engage in social reform, rescue, liberation, empowerment, or treatment? And what type of ideology might support these or other approaches to alleviating poverty and its consequences, or the attainment of social justice? The final answers to these questions won't be found entirely in prescriptions, techniques, lectures, or books. Perhaps there is another place to look for the inspiration needed to pursue these ideals. It is possible that the seeds of concern about unfairness, injustice, and poverty might be the primary incentive of at least some students who have chosen social work as their career. If this is the case, is it the mission of professional education to enable students to become mindful of their latent commitments as at least the first step?

Although thoughtful reflection is an essential principle of all forms of practice, there is a still higher order of professional thinking that can be called *critical reflection* and *analysis*. It is a kind of thought that is concerned not just with an external problem or outlying condition, but with the inner moral beliefs and ideologies of the learner—or perhaps only *some* learners. For in entering the profession of social work, students generally are enacting an ideal, a realization of certain convictions or ideologies. In joining the moral and social mission of the profession, they hope to make a difference in the lives of clients or in the community or the larger systems that affect clients' well-being. As I mentioned at the outset, these inspirations may appear quixotic but are nonetheless compelling.

Courses on poverty and discrimination are necessary and may be enlightening to all students. But such courses do not always provoke students to critically examine what they really stand for. In contrast with the rhetoric and abstractions of the classroom, the practicum is the locale where learners contend with poverty and discrimination not as concepts, but as powerfully toxic conditions directly known and felt by sentient human beings. For example, students find themselves hunting for solutions to the dilemmas of single mothers in a neglected housing project, or those who face exclusion from public welfare support. Other students witness the sorrows of Asian-American children in a public school who are shunned because they are visibly different. To be sure, every prospect for practical help for these individuals must be pursued. But, considering the principled objectives of the CPS, how does one begin to grapple with the moral, cultural, economic, and political environment in which these dismal conditions are embedded? How does one begin to contemplate the balance between personal responsibility and the obligations of society? The mediums for this reflective process of inquiry and action are collegial discourse and critical analysis.

Collegiality implies a kind of two-way street, the sharing of power and authority, the relation that occurs between and among inquiring minds. Thus far, we have given principal attention to only one side of this exchange, the learner; not much has been said about the reciprocal role of the teacher. In addition to the authority of knowledge and pedagogical know-how that the teacher should provide, what else must she or he contribute to the learning experience, especially to the process of education for critical thinking? Paulo Freire (1998), in a posthumous collection of writings, offers some answers to these questions.

Introducing his idea of pedagogy, Freire asserts:

> There is, in fact, no teaching without learning. One requires the other. And the subject of each, despite their obvious differences, cannot be educated to the status of object. Whoever teaches learns in the act of teaching, and whoever learns teaches in the act of learning. (p. 31)

Speaking specifically of the teacher's role, he adds:

> Since I cannot be a teacher without considering myself prepared to teach well and correctly the contents of my discipline, I cannot reduce my teaching practice to the mere transmission of these contents. It is my ethical posture in the course of teaching these contents that will make the difference. It is a posture made up of my commitment to thoroughness, my investment in excellence, and my competent preparation that reveals humility rather than arrogance. It is a posture of unconditional respect for the students, for the knowledge they have that comes directly from life and that,

> together with the students, I will work to go beyond. My coherence in the classroom is as important as my teaching of contents. A coherence of what, I say, write, and do. (p. 94)

Freire cautions against a top-down, authoritative bearing and insists that the teacher must be a careful listener to what students have to say:

> If the structure of my thinking is the only correct one, accepting no criticism, I cannot listen to anyone who thinks or elaborates ideas differently from mine. Neither can I hear the person who speaks or writes outside the norms of accepted standard language. And how is it possible, then to be open to ways of being, thinking, and evaluating that we consider the exotic eccentricities of other cultures?. . . The democratic-minded teacher, aware of the impossibility of neutrality, needs to cultivate a special kind of knowledge that can never be forgotten so as to sustain his or her struggle. It is this: If education cannot do everything, there is something fundamental that it can do. In other words, if education is not the key to social transformation, neither is it simply the means to reproduce the dominant ideology. (pp. 107–110)

If we are indeed serious about fulfilling the noble objectives set forth in the CPS with regard to the well-being of our clients and the promotion of social and economic justice, we should not overlook the legacy of critical thought and action in the work of Jane Addams. Lundblad (1995) in fact, proposes "that Addams's accomplishments could serve as a "role model for the 1990s." In the absence of schools of social work and within the programs of Hull House, Addams inductively devised her own social work methods. Appalling living conditions served as her point of departure as an advocate, organizer, and lobbyist. Addams was the pupil, and her community neighbors were her teachers. She defined Hull House as a living, dynamic educational process, one that worked both ways. As Lunblad suggests, "from this experience she generalized that education ought to be perceived as a mutual relationship between teacher and pupil under the conditions of life and not the transmission of knowledge, intact and untested by experience" (p. 663).

"Conscientization," another term coined by Freire, captures the idea of education for critical thinking. At one point, some 20 years ago, Freire's model of education (1973a, 1973b, 1973c) captured the interest of some social work educators and practitioners. Freire's ideas alerted them to the larger, oppressive political and economic burdens that impeded social justice and opportunity. In his view, the standard designs of education only perpetuated these conditions.

Freire is a central figure in Galper's (1980) book on radical social work, ahead of its time in introducing the now widespread doctrine of empowerment as a goal of helping people. Indirectly, Galper advocated the role of experiential learning at the critical and analytic level. He cited the example (that recalls the efforts of Jane Addams) of a group of students that created its own field placement by setting up their residence in a community. There they not only worked with the neighborhood associations and their projects, but also enlisted the participation of faculty in their enterprise (pp. 240–242).

Teacher as Student/Student as Teacher. Conscientization, or consciousness raising, is the model of education that challenges the banking system approach to education. The basis of this model is experiential or what Freire calls "problem-posing." In this activity, teachers and students as co-investigators of reality engage in mutual and respectful dialogue. Freire believes that as students grapple with real-life problems they will be increasingly challenged and obliged to respond to that challenge. And critical learning deepens even more when students realize that these problems are seriously interrelated with economic, social, and political problems in the larger context. Healthy dialogue dissolves the distinctions between what Freire calls "the teacher-of-the-students" and "the students-of-the-teacher" and new relational terms emerge: "teacher-student" and "student-teacher." They become jointly responsible for a process in which all grow in ways that make possible learning that is liberating, critical, and creative (1973c).

The thawing of the solidified distinctions that isolate teachers from students and vice versa is, of course, an ideal that is hard to reach. Teachers forget the penalties of the disunion of teachers and students and how such division affected their own education. Elizabeth Minnich (1990) reminds us:

> We all speak of Kuhn, and about paradigm shifts, but many somehow do not use that understanding when they feel challenged about their own discipline as an organizing framework that allows them to feel clear about what is and what is not their subject matter. They forget, once they become authorities in their own field, what they knew as graduate students. Generations of graduate students have wended their way through the minefields of interprofessional competition, carefully figuring out which approaches they must use with which professors on which exams lest they get caught in the cross-fire. And yet, once certified, many then proceed to defend their own views of what 'properly' constitutes their discipline with the same totalizing vehemence from which they once suffered. (p. 172)

As Minnich points out, one barrier to a collaborative form of teaching in which the distinction between teacher and student is dissolved occurs when a teacher needs to defend her intellectual territory and resist other possible approaches or disturbing questions offered by students.

Still, without ideals we would have no goals. So let us go forward and consider how these themes are elaborated in a more current educational proposal. David Moore (1990) agrees that critical discourse in experiential education represents one of the few paths toward creating a critical pedagogy. Again, this is a level of education on which teachers and students can openly explore the social institutions, power relations, and value commitments that impinge on services to people and communities. Moore builds on poststructuralist conceptions of knowledge use, ideas proposed by such writers as Michel Foucault and Jurgen Habermas. Briefly put, Foucault opposes knowledge that subjugates rather than frees; Habermas warns against a "false consciousness" that results from the willingness to accept existing social arrangements without critical questions.

Moore poses these important questions: How can we "teach" about experience? What is it that we are teaching? In his search for answers he differentiates between structuralist and poststructuralist approaches to teaching and learning. The structuralist, or traditional, teacher prepares a course with clear-cut objectives that are used as criteria to judge whether students are grasping the issues and facts related to the content of the course. For example, a course focused on child protection services might expect students to learn about related laws, interagency communications, relevant research, family court, and the policies and practices of particular social agencies. This acquired knowledge equips students with a framework they can apply as an explanatory matrix to their field placements. Accordingly, their field observations are then recycled into the classroom as they move toward more advanced teaching and learning. This is useful learning, as far as it goes, but it remains encapsulated by the structure used to guide learning, or what I referred to earlier as a "premature structure." In other words, what is observed and learned likely will not exceed the boundaries of the established structure of knowledge acquired by the learner. What we perceive is limited by what we think we know.

In contrast, poststructuralist learning, or critical discourse, is participatory and in accord with Freire's idea of the teacher-student and student-teacher sharing the same learning experience. Here, the teacher also provides information, but largely to give students a picture of the state of the art and a point of departure for critical analysis. Ultimately, the students, based on their analysis, will teach their teacher about the realities of child protection services. Students are expected to "read" their field placements as "texts" where the story of the setting can be analyzed.

This approach frees students to explore certain details that otherwise might not be included in more formal frameworks. It also urges them to trust their intuitions. Thus, they might explore the history of ideas and ideologies, the unquestioned presumptions that, over time, have come to govern service delivery. Students might be curious about the covert and unquestioned values that the agency perpetuates in its definition of parental responsibility. The role of clients, as reflected in the tacit power arrangements of the agency might be scrutinized. Or students might weigh the merits of prevailing practice theories and their relevance for child protection. The educational goal is not right answers, but rather, the generation of critical questions. Within an open climate of learning, all participants must be free to initiate comments, "challenge truths, and question theories" (Moore,

1990, pp. 280–281). The desired outcome is the discovery of a broader range of interpretations, an analysis of the changes that might be needed, and the goals that might realistically be achieved. On a grander level, beyond the exercise itself, the aim of critical discourse is to develop and strengthen the reflective thinking that will define and redefine effective, competent practitioners.

As a critical thinker, the maturing social worker comes to realize that the lofty intent to alleviate poverty or enhance social justice is perhaps beyond the influence of the individual practitioner, never mind beyond the scope of any one profession. But the option of dismissing such ambitions is not acceptable. Again, as Freire said, "if education cannot do everything, there is something fundamental that it can do." And what the mature learner can do will depend on the passion and imagination freed by a critical and reflective mind. The effects of mature and critical thinking should influence practice itself, whether it involves clients and families, planners, communities, or other systems. Within the spirit of collegiality, critical reasoning can be the means by which participants reconsider and redefine their roles and responsibilities as experts about their own lives and circumstances who can take action to improve their circumstances.

Still, of the many educational lodestars or ideals that we have considered thus far, the mastery of critical reasoning and discourse may be a bit beyond the reach of some learners for some very prosaic reasons. Although it is a crude distinction, we know there are many able students who are very competent and effective "doers" but are less inclined to be "thinkers." I have already mentioned the more convergent thinkers who would not take kindly to what they would see as the lack of structure or focus in dialogue and discourse that is open and free-flowing. For students who look for structure, an emphasis on discussion may seem windy and detached from the real-life problems that concern them.

This distinction is not intended to be pejorative. Gardner's theory of multiple intelligences tells us that within the same profession some learners will gravitate toward one sub-specialty, field, or problem to the exclusion of others. Where one student might value the intimacy and ambiguities of intensive psychotherapy, another student will feel more secure working within the rational strictures of agency administration or planning. In research, some individuals will opt for the clear-cut protocols of quantitative inquiry, while others will be more comfortable wandering the boundless maze of qualitative explorations. Such individual differences are deeply valued in the experiential model of learning, with its many pathways to growth and proficiency. Yet, this doesn't mean that opportunities for critical discourse at some level of thinking should be neglected. It is the responsibility of the mentor to make every learning opportunity count. At the very least, students should always be expected to look at and clarify their interventions, their evaluations, and other choices and activities that characterize their practice. Social workers cannot plod through the quagmire of personal anguish and social inequity only to allow themselves the temptation of facile solutions. Any action that affects lives, relationships, and futures deserves critical reflection and careful judgment.

Experiential Learning in Action: A Case in Point

Now as I shift from an abstract, theoretical view of experiential learning to the actual process as it unfolds in practice, I want to direct attention to the critical, intermediating component of *relationship.* This factor was implicit in the theories and operations covered in the previous section. In real life, however, relationship is the crucial dynamic of learning and change.

Lee Knefelkamp, professor of adult and higher education at Columbia Teachers College, and Carol Schneider, executive vice president, Association of American Colleges and Universities (1997) are advocates of the types of experiential learning represented by Kolb's model. Although they support a shift of focus away from faculty-centered teaching to student-centered learning, they are concerned about overly individualized learning. Knefelkamp and Schneider state that if this should occur,

> learning leaves experiences of social connection and communal obligation on the periphery, beyond the boundaries of the model. *How* the learner may choose to use the newly acquired understanding and intellectual power is an issue left, in this individualized learning model, absolutely elective to the learner. (p. 333)

The importance of relationship and the risk of highly individualized learning will be evident in the case study of one learner and practitioner. Not only does the study portray this learner's encounters with classroom and field learning, but it puts a human face on the speculative ideas we have considered. It also proves that true learning cannot be mapped out with the logic of a course outline, but is more like a quest that calls on personal artistry, talents, and other characteristics. Admittedly, this particular case is an uncommon choice; the narrator of the account, Robin Bouc, is my 24 year old grandson. But bias and selectivity are in play whenever one elects one case over others to illustrate an idea or point. It would be illogical to pick a case to disprove something. Moreover, I believe the candor and trust that characterizes Robin's and my relationship more than compensates for the distance and impartiality lost in such a choice.

Other benefits also accrue from this selection. In a manner of speaking, Robin can be considered close to being a pristine learner. What I mean by this odd term is that he is untouched and unaffected by the scholastic, philosophic, and socializing influences of professional education. Also, Robin's reflections on the influences that motivated him to be a social worker provide some insight into other students' incentives in making such a career choice.

Robin profited from the privilege of a fine undergraduate program in which he enjoyed some limited field experiences. His learning was not influenced by my views on practice. Living on the opposite coasts, our visits are, sadly, too infrequent. To say it simply, Robin's account allows us to vicariously travel with him and gain some insights into what it means to be a natural learner. Robin's account is a result of a chance inspiration. On a visit to the West Coast some months back, Robin eagerly talked about the excitement and rewards of his work as a counselor and care worker at a small, local residential center for mental health patients. He was beginning to believe that he was making some difference in the clients' lives and painted a vivid and compassionate picture of his relationships with his clients and their shared activities. I was captivated by what seemed to be creativity mixed with thoughtful discernment about the nature and needs of his clients. Not knowing what might result, I asked Robin if he would take a stab at writing a kind of autobiography of his educational and professional life, something that might capture what he believed contributed to his process of learning about how to help. I intentionally set no boundaries or guidelines, leaving it to him alone to fashion his story. Months later, I received a report that had been written in occasional moments of reflection on his growth, learning, and practice. I should advise that in preparing his account for inclusion here, I took no liberties with the literal content, but did keep the chronology in order, omitting many reflections that were dispersed throughout the sequence of events he described.

Robin's report begins by recalling his undergraduate education and the content and experience that meant the most to him:

> My last semester of high school was where I completed my first psychology class. That was my first look into human behavior, where I learned about people like Freud and Jung, for example. For the first time subjects and theories of a certain discourse really were "clicking" for me. . . . I knew that I wanted to study psychology and the human services in college.
>
> When I first attended junior college, I took every psychology class that was offered along with cultural anthropology, philosophy, and sociology. These classes pretty much gave me a taste of the existing literature, theories, studies, and the general work done in the intellectual and academic realm. But all these classes combined didn't have nearly the effect on me as did my two-semester field study working one-to-one with a severely ill mental health client. Richard was 46 and diagnosed as paranoid schizophrenic. I discovered he had a true heart of gold. Although he was very slow to trust, we established a trusting relationship after four or five weeks. We would spend four or more hours together on Tuesdays when I picked him up at his residential treatment center. We would plan to do interesting things for each week's meeting. When he had his frequent bouts with delusions, all I could think to do in these instances was what felt right—to just be myself and provide a safe environment with support, encouragement and reality checks, if appropriate. When I spoke on life and ways to deal with its struggles, I could see a change in the way Richard looked at me. What made a difference

> was my supervisor and mentor who gave me basic guidance and would constructively criticize the stories I would share about my time with Richard. Although she was quick to offer suggestions, she always trusted me to be myself, knowing that is where the best work comes from.
>
> When I made the move from junior college to the university I was excited about my new life but sad and feeling guilty about leaving Richard. At the same time it became crystal clear to me that I wanted to pursue social working [*sic*] with this population.

Robin said that his university studies were more focused. He took many upper division psychology classes and found that courses on individuals and groups stimulated him more than the personality, clinical, or developmental models. But most important:

> The majority of my educational achievements at UCSC was [*sic*] reached through introspection not through books, tests, lectures, and papers. I learned a great deal about the different theories within the field of psychology but my main focus was and still is the infinite amount of knowledge to be sought about who I am—my strengths, qualities, gifts, passions, weaknesses and how I can deal with this hectic, complicated world. It was clear to me that so many of the psych majors could really benefit from some serious self-reflection before continuing to move blindly through the educational system.

Robin gained some serious insights when he interned for two quarters at a very structured, group-focused day program for acute mental health clients. He was troubled by the absence of staff-client relations apart from the group itself. There was no "schmoozing" unless staff and clients were smokers who found themselves together at the same smoking spot.

> When in group I always tried to fit in, wear their shoes as much as I could. I felt uncomfortable wearing the formal dress attire I was expected to wear because it distinguished me from my clients. I wanted to understand these disabled, institutionalized people especially as I felt that without understanding there is little healing. And so I would share tidbits of my

> life with the group if appropriate and tried to fit in despite my gelled hair and dress shirt. I suppose I was successful for I was often asked if I was a client. Hanging out with the clients during their breaks, I began to understand the wide array of differences in who they were from their life stories.

Robin was allowed to run his own group, a "young persons" group. He felt it was a success, but his supervisor thought otherwise, as she showed through her criticism ("constructive, of course"). He also started a weekly yoga group that was enjoyable "despite the challenges of getting people who are so 'out' of their bodies to feel more centered 'within' their bodies. It was the beginning of a movement group that I still do today." A major problem was the lack of mentorship and supervision. The staff was overworked and impersonal, a situation which offered scarce opportunities for him to get guidance and feedback from his supervisor and co-workers. Robin felt awkward and insignificant and spent even more time with the residents who

> began to see me as someone special. Someone they could trust and be real with. Seeing this, my supervisor backed even farther away. I was left to figure things out on my own, to sort through all my new experiences, emotions, conflicts, and questions. I kept a journal required by my field study class. It helped me organize my confusion and express my frustration.

With graduation in sight, Robin searched for a mental health facility where he could work. Meanwhile, he volunteered at a drop-in center founded by a former client and staffed by clients who offered peer counseling and other activities. On behalf of the center, he also began doing hospital visits in the locked wards.

> I had no idea why these patients were hospitalized or what their diagnoses was [*sic*]. This experience was very meaningful to me. Sometimes they wanted to talk, other times they wanted advice and had a lot of questions. Sometimes we would just sit together silently. I would draw from my own resources to provide some answers or just share some wisdom. I gained a great deal of confidence from these visits. I was there for them, helping, even counseling, without direction or guidelines. I let my intuition and empathy guide me

on a path of healing and support. There was no one to criticize me. I related to and spoke with these people from my heart and soul: they felt my genuineness.

After graduation, Robin accepted a position at a residential rehabilitation home. "This was very clearly fate for me. My co-workers were shocked at how quickly I learned and how well I fit in. It was the right place and I just flowed with it." It is a large, well-equipped home housing 15 residents. They participate daily in a variety of groups: shopping, art, movement, medication education, and resident council, to name a few. Residents have daily chores, including cleaning and cooking, usually with staff assistance. The staff offers a balance of kindness, discipline, and respect.

We have the freedom to express our individual selves, wear what we want, act naturally and make the center a fun, nurturing place to live and grow for our residents who, ideally, will gain the skills needed to live independently. After a year and a half, I learn every day and still have much more to learn. So much of the wisdom I gain can only be had from experience and exposure. Experience provides the stimulus and allows me to use both intuition and book knowledge to guide my actions. For example, the first time a client confided in me about her suicidal ideation I became highly aware of my self, my words, my actions. Empathy helped me understand what this person needed. I tried to understand what it would be like to feel such despair but still have enough sensibility to seek help from someone. Was it time to give feedback and preach a little, or a time to just listen and be there?

Such experiences provide a backbone, a foundation, for the next situation of this kind. The beauty in experience is that you win either way: a bad decision or mistake can be a blessing if one can learn from it; a good decision shows what is effective. My co-workers are crucial to this learning process. I ask a lot of questions and by discussing alternatives and sharing experience, we are, together, able to create new understanding and awareness. I take each and every experience and create meaning from it. I remain aware of everything I can.

How should we understand Robin's discourse especially in light of the question "How does one learn to become a social worker?" At first glance, one might be inclined to say that his account reveals a certain naivete. And why shouldn't it? Learning that is meaningful is colored by wonder and touched by a sense of revelation. Certainly his words lack the sophistication that one finds in a scholarly treatise. Absent is the lexicon of the profession. He makes no mention of relevant research and pertinent citations. He doesn't speak of "interventions," "theoretical foundations," "assessment," or "systems." But aren't these terms jargon for his otherwise straightforward, unadorned descriptions of his thoughts, understanding, and actions? Robin gives scant attention to the ecological, familial, and other external factors that impinge on the lives of his clients. Robin's approach to his clients is purely of the bottom-up type; he is focused solely on the individual. He starts at square one in his endeavor to fathom both the unique nature of the specific individual and the quality of the emerging relationship between social worker and client. It can be safely assumed that his open and curious mind will gradually admit the many other external forces that allow a deeper and broader understanding of the human condition.

Humanism appears to be Robin's metier for practice. Whatever place the standard psychological theories he gained in his undergraduate classes hold in his thinking, he has moved beyond them to a strong relational, here-and-now approach to his clients. Without reading too much into his account, his approach to his clients tends to parallel a strengths orientation that is committed to the power of personal resilience and the client's potentialities to achieve stability and growth. In addition, he employs the narrative mode as the medium for gaining and providing understanding in the helping relationship. This narrative mode also helps us understand Robin's qualities as a learner and practitioner. In many ways, his manner of practice is more literary than psychological or sociological. In other words, he tends to see people as actors or personages who have stories to tell about their existence rather than as categorical patients, victims, or personality types.

Howard Gardner's framework of personal intelligences and the outline of styles of learning are useful in the attempt to characterize Robin as a learner. The ease with which he makes a trusting and caring relationship possible speaks to his interpersonal talents. His chronicle of learning and practice represents the pursuit of a greater personal awareness or intrapersonal knowledge. His linguistic intelligence allows Robin to express experience and events in vivid and expressive terms. Apparently such skills also provide the language that gives meaning to his exchange with his clients. And he draws from his bodily-kinesthetic attributes to literally embody the helping experience by means of yoga and movement techniques. But as I suggested previously, these talents or intelligences are not employed in the discrete or specialized methods of a technician. Rather, they blend into the whole he presents to his clients.

Correspondingly, Robin implies that his style of practice is largely divergent; he is able to move from the phenomenological particulars of the person or event to contemplate their broader and varied meanings. Even his early work with the delusional mental patient, Richard, shows his artistry in how he moves beyond the blunt diagnosis to its many meanings. Still, when appropriate, Robin can call on convergent modes to focus clients' behaviors on the prosaics of everyday living.

Robin also epitomizes the eccentric dance of experiential learning that follows the rhythms of chance and opportunity. In his internship at the structured day treatment center, he sensed through reflective observation the costs of its rigid and confining climate. Observation of the concrete experience confirmed his impressions and spurred him to find more genuine ways of relating to his clients (active experimentation). His writing about his experience in his journal and the report reflect his efforts at abstract experimentation.

Robin's descriptions of the four settings in which he gained newly found knowledge and competence suggest the many ways in which context shapes the learning experience in affective, perceptual, cognitive, and behavioral terms. His delicately balanced relationship with Richard, essentially raw and devoid of boundaries, helped him understand that he would need to learn how to define the limits of what he knew and how he might help. In this instance, his sensitivity to the uneasy emergence of trust served to provide guidance and direction for his tenuous role of a caring helper. In contrast, his movement into the rigidly structured day program revealed that his emerging style of practice was at variance with the norms of the program and its staff. He found that rules defining and setting apart the behavioral roles of helper and client inhibited his open and self-disclosing approach to his clients. His process of learning continued as he ventured into the locked ward of a hospital and engaged one of the lonely patients. Although walls and locks constrain, he found the opportunity to make the most of his talents, to rise above hard and sterile barriers and fill the need for personal contact and empathy. His current position, in a context that values and encourages openness interwoven with careful discipline and specific objectives, as well as shared discourse and critique among co-workers, has provided Robin with open-ended opportunities to learn, reflect, and mature as a professional. Robin remarks, "Everyone is in a position to learn more, even clients, who can better understand their own illness and how they can help others deal with theirs."

Robin's autobiography traces an ever branching path that begins in the bare passion for learning and for being of service to people in need. If we think of the previous section as a map of the ideal progression of experiential learning and teaching, Robin gives us but one account of how that unfinished and circuitous journey was actually made. His point of departure, academic education offered him the knowledge, the intellectual grounding and guide for his still tentative career choice. But his experience in the practice settings he selected enabled him to test the integrity of his choice and his talents and aptitudes for carrying it forward. To be sure, mentors and supervisors aided in the process of integration. Those whose presence and commitments were available to him strengthened his aspirations. Others, who were less dependable, proved to him that he also needed to be self-reliant.

The outcome of good experiential learning involves not only an informed and skillful practice but the ability to reflect on the meaning and import of what one knows and does in anticipation of the unknowns that lie ahead. Robin engages in this kind of reflection throughout his report. Speaking about what he has come to understand about professional practice, he says:

> I am realizing lately that the field of social work contains few *true* guidelines. Much of the work is what you make it out to be. Actually, I am just required to give medications, do my paperwork, run groups, and make sure my people have completed their daily chores But my job description does not include about 70 % of what I give, such as my intense desire to help those in need, my positive energy expressed as often as I am able, and my motivation to be creative with clients and really give to them what comes from within.

Another example of this kind of reflection expresses his awareness of something that can be called professional conscience that involves personal discipline and ethical considerations.

> One cannot lose sight of the boundaries and their importance of course. For example, there is the possibility that delusional or psychotic thinking or behavior is affecting interaction—always a challenge. There are many ways to deal with this, many therapeutic techniques can be used. This is fine as long as you are caring enough, genuine enough to remain real.

But from his humanistic perspective he wonders just how impermeable these boundaries should be.

> Clearly it is not "professional" to love or be loved by a client, and they certainly cannot be your "friend" according to guidelines set by the helping professions. I understand the importance of this philosophy: however, if a relationship between two humans anywhere in the world is to be nourishing to either person, there must certainly be something akin to loving and friendliness involved. Indeed, many clients need structure, discipline, and even scolding: even this can be done with love. . . without love there is no healing.

And so, how far has Robin come in his ability to define himself and his work with people? In his words:

> When I first began working in the field I knew that in order to ever help these troubled people, or at least provide support, I must hear their stories. I must know how they feel about their diagnoses, the medications they take, the mental health services they receive, and the social workers, psycholo-

gists, and psychiatrists who "manage" their "cases."

It feels very natural to me, and easy, to make connections with people who practically can't help but be genuine. I constantly strive to be, and pride myself on being, a "real" person. When I talk with my clients I try to avoid superficiality. This may mean something as simple as eye contact or body language expressed in a way that shows that my guards are down and my mind is open. I acknowledge their symptoms in a non-discriminatory fashion, even when the symptoms are profound. I use every resource I have to avoid bias, to focus on the human being before me, as she or he is at that moment. I want for this person to momentarily forget about the client/staff or mentally ill/non–mentally ill dichotomy and really allow the human-to-human relationship blossom and grow.

There are many techniques and methods that can be used to establish a relationship of trust and respect among clients and their workers. I continue to learn more from each experience I have in my relationships with my clients and the others I work with. But basically, to care for others, you must first listen to them whether through talking or looking at their art work, or even sitting together quietly, listening to their silence. Being open to whom [*sic*] they are and what they have to share is the essence of listening.

On summing up, Robin acknowledges that he is young, has much to learn and that "soon I will need graduate education to keep me growing and properly stimulated in this field." One must hope that professional education will not dim or blunt his natural ardor for learning.

Four
Experiential Learning in Social Work Education: Experiments and Programs

Experiential Learning Programs: Beginnings and Variations in the Helping Professions

In its varied educational settings, experiential learning has acquired other titles. Where the term "service learning" refers to the function of experiential learning, "inquiry and action" and "problem-focused learning" indicate the stimulus, and "student-centered learning" names the person who is at the core of the learning experience. Over the 30 years or so of its existence as an educational philosophy and method, experiential learning has had many advocates—most recently David Lempert in his articulate book, *Escape from the Ivory Tower: Student Adventures in Democratic Experiential Education* (1996). Echoing the ideas of John Dewey, Paulo Freire, Howard Gardner, and others, Lempert speaks about the "thinking curriculum." This curriculum is based on the assumption that learning is inseparable from motivation, that it is enhanced by cooperative methods, and more effectively achieved through problem solving and participation than through rote abstraction. Lempert (1996) asserts that students learn best when they enjoy what they are doing, when learning is an adventure rather than a repetitive chore, and when they are motivated by positive incentives rather than through fear. He notes that democracy starts with the individual, at the grass roots and in democratic experiential education where students have the opportunity to participate in their own learning by contributing to the design of the learning experience. Lempert goes on to argue that teachers should be thought of as facilitators, and evaluation should be based on a contractual arrangement. Finally, responsiveness and accountability to the community are for him major criteria of a successful educational process.

Although social workers are often critical of the reductionism and depersonalization of the "medical model," it is interesting that we find the first major efforts to humanize education, to awaken social consciousness, occurring within medical education. The impetus for this endeavor to transform medical education was the McMaster Model, originated in the mid-1960s at the Faculty of Medicine at McMaster University in Hamilton, Ontario (Camp, 1999). Concerned that the academic culture of medical education was graduating doctors with inadequate compassion, common sense, and ethical awareness, the faculty instituted problem-based learning. From their first day in medical school, students gathered in small groups with a real patient to diagnose the patient's condition and prescribe a course of treatment. With the ongoing guidance of a mentor, students drew from their own knowledge, feelings, and intuitions and from the multiple intelligences of group members. As students became accustomed to experiential learning, they began to understand the values and meaning of their education. Not only did compassion and ethics improve but their competence grew as well. In the ensuing years, the McMaster Model was adopted by other medical schools in Europe, Australia, and the United States.

A variation of the McMaster Model exists at the Medical School at Case Western Reserve University, Cleveland, Ohio, where the educational goal for the student is to acquire the skills to solve clinical problems scientifically, humanistically, and with benefit to the patient. The educational approach is distinguished by traditions of openness, collegiality, and continuing self-renewal. The intellectual environment is one in which students have the opportunity to demonstrate initiative and responsibility for their own education. Small group learning is emphasized. The student is taught through case study. The aim is to produce doctors who look at patients as human beings for whom illness may have a profound socioeconomic and emotional impact.

Students in this program are, at the very outset, involved in direct experience with patients in the Family Care Program (Curriculum Handbook, 1997-1998: III 2-3). Early in the first year of medical school, each student is assigned to a pregnant woman. The student has the opportunity to observe and support the patient through her prepartum course and delivery. After the patient has given birth, the student is expected to be accessible to the patient. The student is the principal liaison to the physicians caring for the patient and as such is part of the patient's health care team. Workshops help prepare the student for the Family Care experience and an interviewing program is designed to help students communicate effectively with patients.

Following a gradual adoption of experiential, problem-based, or student-centered learning by some medical schools during the 1970s and 1980s, there has been an enormous growth in use of this educational method (Camp, 1999). For instance, at Simon Fraser Faculty of Education (Burnaby, British Columbia), students at the outset are teamed in pairs and assigned to a classroom teacher who carries the title "School Associate." Students generally begin working with single students, gradually increasing their range of teaching to include small groups and finally whole class teaching. This experience is supported by a course in which students study the literature of education and engage in seminars that examine the educational issues that bear on their practicum experiences. An important goal of the combined experiences is for students to find meaning in the vast and complex world of educational practice and to have this meaning informed by extensive study of the literature. In addition, students are expected to develop the ability to assess their professional development by means of thoughtful and reflective discourse. School Associates and Faculty Associates are involved in the supervision of student teachers, usually in three-way conferences.

In addition to problem-based and student-centered learning, *service learning* is a kind of experiential learning. Operating largely at the undergraduate level of higher education, service learning combines a more effective method of teaching than non–service learning and presents students the challenge of integrating what they learn across disciplines. It is also designed to foster social responsibility, intercultural understanding, research skills, critical thinking, and ethical reasoning through service to communities (Kupiec, 1993). The goals of service learning are various: to fill the unmet needs of communities; to enable students to help and enter caring relationships with others; to develop an environment of collegial participation among students, faculty, and community; to expose students to societal inadequacies and injustices; and to help students see the relevance of the academic subject to the real world (Florida International University Digital Library, 1999). That service learning is an established institution in its own right is evident in the growing body of literature that supports its educational philosophy and method. (see *Michigan Journal of Community Service Learning* from the University of Michgan; see also Ostrow, Hesser, & Enos, 1999).

Although the aforementioned examples illustrate there is no universal model of experiential education, they are all based on a common set of assumptions about how students learn and the merits of a problem-focused, hands-on, individualized, student-centered, and discovery approach to learning. The particular methods used will depend on many educational variables. In medical education, for example, students obviously need to learn and incorporate a vast amount of scientific and technical knowledge to complement and inform their practical and humanistic work with patients. In contrast, the teacher education program at Simon Fraser is practicum-centered rather than classroom-centered. In other words, the academy serves as an adjunct to the field. Academic knowledge is a conceptual resource that learners can rely on and draw from to provide the needed structure and theory for their evolving teaching skills. Conversely, in the case of service learning, community work serves to enrich and give meaning to students' primary classroom education. Other variables that affect the form of experiential education include the inspiration and commitments of faculty, the investment of the educational institution, the recipients of services, the nature of the special communities, and the talents and motivations of the learner.

Experiential Learning in Social Work Education

Despite its various permutations within different disciplines and professions, the experiential model of education has not been embraced in social work education in the United States. It is clearly not a priority in the Council on Social Work Education's Curriculum Policy Statement or in its publications. If indeed this approach is being tested in certain educational programs, one finds little in the professional literature to attest to such endeavors. The literature I have cited in these pages, and the occasional articles on field teaching that appear in the *Journal of Education for Social Work* and *Journal of Teaching in Social Work*, are all premised on the firm and traditional separation of class and field. However, despite the lack of interest in experiential education in social work programs in the United States, experiential education has developed its own domain in certain programs in England and Australia.

My first encounter with experiential education occurred nearly 25 years ago. The setting was the Maritime School of Social Work at Dalhousie University in Halifax, Nova Scotia, where, after teaching in two American social work programs, I accepted a position as chair of the practice sequence. Although I was not exactly a stranger in a strange land, it gradually dawned on me that whatever Canadian social work was at that time, it was in some important respects different from U.S. social work. To be sure, the bond between the two countries was secure. Canadian social work used the term "North American" social work to acknowledge this bond without having constantly to refer to the United States and thereby suffer loss to its own identity.

I learned my lesson from the faculty of the social policy sequence who turned out to occupy a political position somewhat to the left of policy people in mainstream U.S. schools. They fought ardently to replace the emphasis on the individual in the school's mission statement with an emphasis on the social or communal. In addition, they wished to extend the communal, democratic, and equal rights doctrine to the operations and structure of the educational program by granting students equal rights with faculty. In brief, the goal of social work in their view was not individual treatment but social care, social justice, and community service, an argument that Specht and Courtney (1994) affirmed years later in their book, *Unfaithful Angels*, a landmark in social work literature.

This educational climate prompted me to experiment with revising two of the established educational routines. One involved the procedures for placing students in field settings; the second dealt with creating new structures for field placements themselves. In accord with principles of democratic participation (and, as I now appreciate, individual learning needs and styles), students were invited to seek out and contract for field placements they believed would be most meaningful and inspiring in relation to their interests and career plans. By no means was this a carte blanche venture; a working contract with approved supervision and a clear statement of educational goals were required. The negotiations to achieve these changes required time and careful attention but quickly proved to be fruitful. In many instances, the innovative nature of the students' choices inspired faculty to serve as supervisors.

When presented with the opportunity to choose field placements, students divided themselves into two groups. The first group was comprised of those who were immediately excited and inspired by the opportunity to design their own learning experience. The second group included those who were far more reticent, those who believed they were unprepared to make such a critical choice and would therefore depend on more authoritative judgments. Now that I am armed with the appropriate terminology, I can look back and see how individual talents and learning styles influenced their choices. The more divergent and creative thinkers among the students, and those who were somewhat experienced in the field, readily opted for the more autonomous choice. Less experienced students and those who were more comfortable with directed learning tended to rely on their advisors' recommendations for field placements.

The students who didn't want to choose their placements were assigned to the school's familiar and established settings: mental health clinics, hospitals, and other social service agencies. The students who embraced the choice of field placements set up shop in an array of mostly nontraditional settings that offered access to learning opportunities that fit learning styles and career interests. For example, one student worked closely with the regional head of the New Democratic Party, a Canadian political party espousing a social democratic philosophy. Another student joined the editorial staff of an underground newspaper, reporting and publishing stories on people and communities struggling with certain social hardships. A third worked with Amnesty International dealing with human rights abuses. A few students helped develop hotlines for runaway children, rape crisis, and information for the elderly. Public residences for the aging, the city's social planning department, and the police department rounded out the other choices. What meant the most to these students was the sense that they "owned" their placements; they were fully invested in both their learning and the aims and purposes of the setting itself.

The same balance of interests carried over into a subsequent plan that encouraged a group of students to pioneer a new freestanding placement in a locale where social and other general services were deficient or absent. The students, guided and supervised by a faculty member, found a challenging target: the town of Sackville, a bedroom suburb of Halifax. The Sackville Project proved to be a virtual paradigm of experiential learning. The first stage of concrete experience occurred as the students hit the streets in search of information and impressions that would help them shape the questions they needed to ask. They discovered a number of ironies that would not have been evident in the top-down planning. First, the locus of power in the community was not among the established authorities of the town; it was the local undertaker who had the real story and who could be counted on for advice. Likewise, they found that the most pressing problems were those of the voiceless—the aging, children, and single mothers. It seemed that these residents had, for one thing, resigned themselves to the lack of public transportation. As a result, appointments with physicians or other service providers were out of reach, and chances to shop for food and medicines were few and far between.

With a more precise understanding of the most pressing needs and problems of the community, the students and their mentor could deliberate about the most practical methods necessary to implement certain plans. They had the eager support of the parish priest. And the principal of the elementary school invited them to position their field placement in the school where they had access to children and their families. From this point on the students took charge, identified and worked with community consultants, and set up a volunteer transportation program. The scope of their efforts broadened as the community recognized them as a resource for meeting a variety of social and personal needs.

I cannot say that this remarkable learning experience had any significant effect on the university social work program itself. The lack of any conceptual grounding or argument for this approach to education combined with the absence of any incentive to alter the program's structure or traditional teaching methods meant that the Sackville Project was considered a fascinating innovation or an interesting novelty. Certainly, it had no lasting effect. As we know, innovations of this kind are often the brainchild and the passion of an individual or small team. Should the spark fade so will the original plan.

Now to describe three experimental educational programs that have endured. All three were founded on principles of experiential learning, and each has published scholarly accounts of its particular project. I am also aware of other programs that have at times experimented with various aspects of experiential learning. One form involves classroom faculty who teach or supervise in the field. In another instance, students have been placed within a consortium of social services for special populations (aging, child welfare). In this program the field teacher helps to integrate a range of learning experiences over the spectrum of services. And there are many projects designed to better integrate class and field education. In these examples, the traditional separation of the classroom and the field remained intact.

It is also important to note the alternative pathway towards improved experiential learning based on Rogers's (1996) study of the British system of social work education. This pathway conforms to the traditional class-field arrangement. Rogers's recommendation that field teachers should receive extended special training and accreditation deserves the attention of all educators. Rogers observes that the social work literature of the United States, Canada, and the United Kingdom expresses concern that field education is a neglected area of social work education—one often marginalized in terms of curricula, staffing, and resource priorities.

Rogers does not use the term "experiential." Still, the skills and educational responsibilities that she attributes to those whom she calls (using the more apt British term) "practice teachers" readily correspond to the skills and responsibilities of those in the role of the mentor in an experiential learning mode. She argues that the core qualities of effective practice teaching lie in the practice teacher's own competence as a practicing social worker. Students learn best from teachers who are clear and confident enough about their own practice skills and knowledge to be able to adapt their teaching to students' learning needs and styles. This ability helps to individualize the student in accord with the basic principles of experiential learning.

Rogers recommends that a course of training for field instructors should extend beyond the information usually given to them on the school's objectives and curriculum. Training should cover the knowledge and skills necessary to teach competent practice, and the methods by which students learn professional skills and values. Training should also include information bearing on issues of culture, diversity, and discrimination and the skills necessary to supervise and evaluate student progress. Rogers concludes that the results of this training program in the UK are impressive, despite the initial fear that the demands of the accreditation system would reduce the number of practice teachers. It was thought that some might be selected out, others would not be allowed release time, and still others might be deterred by the demanding expectations. Instead, the number of practice teachers who feel more competent and less marginalized increased. Furthermore, there was an increase in the number of placements, and partnerships between educational institutions and social service organizations improved.

Enquiry and Action Learning: Bristol University (UK)

The Enquiry and Action Learning (EAL) program inaugurated by Bristol University in the early 1990s is a good example of the fundamentals of the experiential learning model. As the following illustration shows, the basic element of the EAL course is its study unit. Each unit is developed from case scenarios provided by practitioners and agencies. They reflect the situations, problems, and issues that are typical of a locale. In contrast with the traditional didactic method in which information and theory are provided, students themselves discover, in accord with the principles of experiential learning, what they need to know, where they might find this knowledge, and how it might be integrated. Recalling Freire's ideal of teacher as learner and learner as teacher, collegiality is the keystone of this learning experience. The fourfold aims of EAL in effect sum up the expectations of experiential learning. First is the endeavor to draw classroom and field into a harmonious relationship so as to achieve a firmer integration of theory and practice. The second is a consequence of the first: the development of a closer partnership between the school and field work agencies. Third is the creation of a learning environment and group interaction that is better suited to the diverse learning needs and attributes of adults entering into professional education. And the fourth is explicit preparation for collaboration in professional teams.

Burgess and Jackson (1990) describe how students are introduced to EAL. A group listens to a recording of a phone call from a health visitor to a social services department. The caller is concerned about an 84-year-old woman who has been found by her neighbor wandering the streets. The students discuss their first reaction to the call. One student is concerned about the neighbor interfering, another relates the scenario to her parents' troubling situation, and a third talks of her previous job arranging residential care for the elderly. Other students speak of their apprehension about what they might do since they lack experience with elderly people. Guided by the faculty facilitator, the student group ponders the kinds of skills and knowledge they would need to understand the situation and take effective action. Their list includes questions about social policy and services available to the elderly, ethical questions related to self-determination, and the social, physiological, and psychological causes of the woman's confusion. They also list the powers, authority, and duties of the social worker, cultural differences in family responsibility, how one best communicates with the elderly; and how to make third party referrals.

The students then work out their learning priorities and the resources available to them, like books, videos, and consultation with practitioners and other students. At the next meeting with the facilitator, the students share the fruits of their research, and with this information reconsider the phone call and work out some action plans that should be taken. Evaluation is an important phase of this process as they critically appraise their activities, identifying their achievements and difficulties in working effectively both individually and as a group. They offer feedback about the usefulness of this form of study, the quality of available resources, and the collegial role of the facilitator.

Many of us are familiar with the fact that the best and bravest of plans to revise curriculum, course content, or teaching methods do not readily translate into action. The rhetoric of a plan, no matter how well its rationale gets worked out, does not come alive like a recipe in the hands of a cook or the architectural blueprint used by a contractor. Thus there are lessons to be learned in the reflections of Hilary Burgess (1992), one of the major authors of the EAL plan. These lessons illuminate the human and systemic foibles that are encountered along the path of planning and implementation.

Writing about "swimming upstream," Burgess recalls that the timing for the implementation of the plan was not the best. The political and economic climate in England contributed to immense pressure and a scarcity of resources that made it difficult to take on the new roles and responsibilities required by such a radical shift in the philosophy of education. But the student interest and energy for learning sparked during the very first week of the program lightened the initial troubles. As Burgess (1992) remarks, "They seemed to dive into their learning, returning to study group meetings laden with ideas and notes and books and a desire to tell their colleagues about it all." Central to the success of EAL was a problem-based approach. Students were interested in part because they said to themselves, "This is something I'm likely to come across, something I need to find out about" (pp. 109–111).

The field agencies offered no resistance to the plan because of the past spirit of cooperation that marked school and community relationships. But the university administration was another matter. The inauguration of a plan as radical as EAL runs counter to traditions of teaching where the expert teacher imparts his or her learning to passive students. But as in many cases, economic pressures and political influence were used to short-circuit objections to the proposed educational reforms. The pressing economic conditions led administrators to be receptive to ideas which in other circumstances they might reject. And fortunately there was another unforeseen political advantage. At the time of the program proposal the chair of the social work program was also serving in a high-level administrative position in the university, which meant greater access to key individuals and committees.

The uncertainty of social work faculty involved in the EAL program was a major concern. As Burgess observes, few academics feel comfortable or well prepared with learning material about which they are not confident. Although mutual support was enabling, the novel role of facilitator stirred persistent questioning. Faculty were perplexed, for example, about how active and directive they were expected to be in leading a study group. They were also puzzled by the variability of facilitator style. Was there a "right" way to facilitate? Here, awareness of group process and dynamics was helpful, considering that, whatever the style of the facilitator, its effects on the group always should be open to discussion.

In her concluding thoughts (pp. 119–120), Burgess makes a critical point: the hardest part of the EAL program was not so much its implementation as it was keeping its course true to the educational philosophy. For there were constant efforts to revert to more traditional and familiar forms of teaching. In some instances students or agency staff felt the need for the usual didactic input in order to be assured that this topic or that one was properly "covered." In the long run Burgess was secure about her belief that the EAL approach was a culmination of her work with communities involving principles of participation, empowerment, self-direction, and support. "As with all community work, the true test will come not just with time, but with the personal stories of those involved—the students. We wait to hear their voices."

The voices of these students and other evaluations of the program were heard soon thereafter in *The Quality Assessment Report for the Applied Social Work Program* by the Higher Education Funding Council of England (HEFCE, 1994). The report spoke of the impressive levels of high-quality student participation that demonstrated their ability to use their own experience and awareness of contemporary research to make useful contributions to the progress of the group as a whole. Both students and staff demonstrated skillful facilitation and leadership, clear planning and setting of objectives, clear command of material, an atmosphere of trust within the group, and supportive encouragement for students to develop at their own pace. In general staff-student relations were characterized by a friendly, adult working climate.

Finally, a broad range of measures was used to gather information about the program's effectiveness. Democratic learning was clearly evident in the large amount and high quality of student feedback in written and oral forms. The strong commitment to student representation provided more evidence of democratic learning. The range of student work was noteworthy. Students acquired a range of specialist and generalist skills, and genuine integration was realized. As a final measure of success applications to the program doubled from the previous two years.

Problem Based Learning: University of Newcastle, New South Wales, Australia

In the Department of Social Work at Newcastle the model of problem-based learning is situated within a *strengths* perspective. This perspective is seen as a major means of integrating the theory, practice, and values of social work for all students. In its implementation of problem-based learning the social work program was strongly supported by the university, which has an overall commitment to the problem-based approach. Every department is grounded in this model of learning.

In "Preparing Social Workers for an Uncertain Future," English, Gaha, and Gibbons (1994) point out some interesting and critical perspectives on the problem-based approach to experiential learning. They mention a drawback to using the term "problem." It has been given negative connotations in the social sciences, where a problem is something to be remedied or treated therapeutically. As a result, it is too easy to see clients as "different," a judgment usually made by those who have "expert" authority. The authors recommend a shift from a "problem-saturated" to a "solution focused," or strengths approach.

The organizing principle for learning is the learners' experiences, a wellspring of wisdom derived not only from the classroom and field but their personal life experiences as well. The latter might include critical transitions in their lives, how and where they lived, and the meanings they extracted from important group events. The acquisition of appropriate knowledge and skills is necessary but not sufficient. Students are also expected to gain awareness of themselves, their beliefs, and their values to build the confidence necessary to act competently and take responsibility for ongoing learning. Fostering (and no doubt, nurturing) students' competence and confidence is a major tenet of the program.

To put this another way, learning involves the whole person: although cognition and intellectual enterprise are important, expectations, desires, emotions, even posture and somatic responses are embodied in learning and practice. English and colleagues (1994) reiterate the stages of experiential learning covered earlier in this book (e.g., exploration and discovery, critical reasoning and analysis). They stress the importance of communication skills and interventions that are sensitive to substantive contextual and ethical matters, and of a professional approach that is always alert to organizational and systemic factors.

An exciting and bold earmark of the program is its accent on creativity. Students are not only encouraged to be creative in problem-solving tasks (brainstorming, experimenting with new ideas, testing different strategies) but they are prepared for the eventuality that they will make mistakes that can reveal fresh insights and new solutions. More than an abstraction, the emphasis on creativity is supported by creative and artistic workshops involving drama and art in which the objective is to overcome the usual habits and routines of thinking. Although the authors do not specifically refer to them, Howard Gardner's concept of several intelligences are virtually evident in students' reports that such opportunities free them to take risks, to pursue new ideas, and to discover newfound personal talents in learning and practice. As was the case in the Bristol program, students democratically and vigorously participate in decision making, including evaluation of the program, teaching, field, and their own performance. One outcome led to the recognition that students have different learning styles. This resulted in a determined effort to encourage "a style of practice unique to each person" (English et al., 1994, p. 293).

Team teaching based on social group work knowledge and skills is an integral component of the experiential learning program (Gibbons, 1992). This approach involving the entire faculty of the program suggests that it serves as an exemplar or model for the study groups comprising facilitators and students.

The staff as a group is responsible for planning learning unit goals and themes for each year. A considerable amount of time is spent at the outset thinking through and discussing the values, beliefs, and concepts critical to social work with the goal of providing a sense of "ownership" and commitment to the Newcastle program. Careful attention is given to the sharing of power in teams. And as is the case in the student study units, opportunities for shared learning and the development of new skills to strengthen the idea that both faculty and students will be engaged in a lifetime of learning. In effect, the team serves as a medium not only for achieving a common purpose in education, but also as a vital and effective means for overcoming the stumbling blocks that frequently arise among educators, conflicts, competition, and sometimes petty issues.

Again, I want to move from rhetoric to reality to show how the ambitious ideals elaborated by the Newcastle program actually pan out. Just one example illustrates how a social work curriculum based on experiential learning helps students to discover their ability to deal with societal inequality (Flynn, 1997). In many ways, it also returns us to the question I raised earlier in response to the CSWE Curriculum Policy Statement requirement that students be prepared to try to "alleviate poverty, oppression, and discrimination" and to "further the well-being of people and promote social and economic justice." The CPS has little to say about the professional knowledge, leverage, and skill required to deal with, or for that matter even think about, ethical and moral problems of such magnitude and complexity. Recall that I proposed that students needed to develop the art of critical reflection and analysis. If this can be accomplished, at least some students may discover their personal beliefs and convictions about human rights and justice. These can serve them well as motivations for thought and action. Let us consider how the Newcastle program puts these ideas in practice.

As a foundation for social work practice focused on the well-being of groups, communities, individuals and families, Newcastle requires "learning experiences to be structured around large, complex situations rather than solvable and simplistic problems." Citing Bawden (1987), Flynn (1997, p. 22) agrees that a preoccupation with "problems" as a structure for learning succeeds only in reducing complex societal situations into what look like simple, manageable replicas of real life. As a result, students will erroneously assume that they should gain mastery over these problems. Social workers of the future will need instead vision and inspiration as well as the courage and imagination to devise alternative and often radical solutions at both individual and structural levels.

Although social justice issues are central to the program, Flynn recognizes that not all students come into social work education with an understanding of, or a commitment to, the profession's mission of social justice. Thus, the process of learning for practice has to somehow confront students with the strength of their own values and how these values will help or hinder their judgments. Throughout the Newcastle program students analyze political contexts and explore options for the pursuit of social justice goals while becoming increasingly aware of how their own values and positions in society influence the process of analysis and reflection. In the third year of the four-year program, students augment this classroom learning with experiential learning through participation in the Criminal Justice System Learning Unit.

Flynn introduces the concept of the "trigger experience" in which the learner comes face-to-face with a special aspect of a situation frequently encountered in social work practice. This metaphor corresponds with what Kolb termed concrete experience, a learning stage where the learner "sees" a set of circumstances in a way that energizes reflection on its meaning. The trigger experience for the criminal justice system learning unit that Flynn (1997) describes was a visit to a police station to learn about the operations of the Child Mistreatment Unit run by the police. The aim of this trigger experience was to stir students' awareness of their own frames of reference and to provoke inquiry into this new area of study. With the intent of critically analyzing the dominant ideological substructure of the legal system, students began to explore the link between the law and inequality in society. They explored the social construction of crime, the various societal responses to crime. They also sought to understand the connections between social work and criminal justice. Ultimately, the "problem" presented to the learning unit was the way the legal system creates or reinforces inequality. Through resources that included various skills workshops as well as information exchange and discussion with legal practitioners and panels of experts, students investigated the relationship between law and inequality.

One of the major outcomes of this educational experience included learning how to use the media to convey information about social injustice to educate the public on discrimination. Working with the university radio station, students gained skills in interviewing, scripting, radio research, and production. Another outcome was the development of confidence and skills necessary for making contact with people whom the students previously regarded as too important to give social workers any of their time. They successfully arranged interviews with significant legal figures, academics, and politicians. Informal contacts with judges allowed students to share their own concerns about the legal system and gain a deeper understanding of the role of the judiciary. Disregarding the aura of power that can discourage challenges to authority, the students became more aware of assertive action as a potential strength for social workers. Ongoing criticism, formal and informal feedback, group processing, and the use of journals strengthened and validated their capabilities.

While not surprisingly the Newcastle students didn't achieve the impossible aim of eradicating social injustice, their achievements went a long way towards preparing them to tackle and improve situations across a range of complexity. The learning activities of the Newcastle students encouraged them to use critical reflection and analysis, kinds of thought concerned both with an external problem or outlying condition and with the inner moral beliefs and ideologies of the learner. It is this kind of learning that will best prepare students to contend with the deep-set social injustices, prejudice and other inequities affecting their clients and thereby make a meaningful difference in those clients' lives.

The Nontraditional Field Placement: University of Kansas School of Social Welfare

The School of Social Welfare at the University of Kansas is another example of an effort to provide opportunities for experiential learning. This effort grew out of a project designed to reach out to consumers who were typically underserved by traditional helping systems. The project involved applying principles of experiential learning within nontraditional placements. Saleebey (1997), the author of a report on the project, believes that such placements not only empower students, but also empower the people they are helping.

Two field settings were created. One was at a public housing project, and the other was in mobile crisis services for deinstitutionalized mentally ill clients. In both instances, faculty served as field instructors. This endeavor was not premised on the provision of services alone. It was envisioned as an opportunity for students to discover how to learn, and what to learn, to recapture the traditional role of social work in responding to problems of poverty, social justice, and discrimination. The project was also designed to show the educational value of substantive experiential learning principles.

Drawing on Dewey's and Piaget's work and the models elaborated by Kolb and others, Saleebey stresses the importance of "learning centeredness," "learner control," and "personal development" as key factors in experiential learning. He cites Weil and McGill's (1989) argument that experiential learning reaches parts of the person that other courses might miss, because it puts identification and development of personal attributes (or the talents or intelligences discussed earlier) directly at the heart of the learning experience. According to Saleebey, such learning provides

> opportunities to explore new ways of being in the world; to recognize unproductive patterns in our ways of responding; to learn that what we say and do may be contradicted by our behavior; to change old ways of responding to interpersonal situations; and to affirm aspects of ourselves which are perhaps undervalued. (p. 16)

Such opportunities are, of course, in accord with Paulo Freire's motif of conscientization, since personal development that springs from experiential learning can generate group consciousness, which can lead to critical consciousness, community action, and social change.

After outlining the educational and service benefits of the nontraditional field unit, Saleebey describes the placements. He carefully delineates the structure, composition, and organization of the public housing social work unit established in cooperation with a specific Tenant Management Corporation (TCM). Planning with the TCM Board commenced three months before the first students arrived, to prepare students for their entry into the unit.

In the first setting, the students lost no time in meeting the difficulties of life in public housing head on. Their immediate learning objectives included the prevention of unjust evictions, meeting emergency assistance needs, and counseling in response to substance abuse and domestic violence. In addition they offered the organizational training required to increase the credibility and effectiveness of the Tenant Membership Board.

In the second setting, the Mobile Crisis Team was designed to provide critical case management to individuals with severe and persistent mental illness who were living in the community. Based on a strengths model of practice, students visited the consumers' residences to assess consumers' personal and environmental strengths and goals and to join with the consumers to work out a plan of action.

Saleebey's observations of the experiences of the two units give new meaning to "the enormous range of complexity" of situations encountered in nontraditional field settings. The situations were characterized by pervasive uncertainty and an exceptional variety and complexity of consumer/client needs. Moreover, based on their past experiences with social service providers, the consumers were very doubtful about the units' intentions. Drawing from these observations, Saleebey offers a number of caveats relative to planning for nontraditional placements. Most noteworthy is the need for the involvement of all key players in all phases of the program. In addition, students must be carefully prepared to engage in the learning process by developing an orientation to and a deep appreciation of the personal and cultural factors that shape the community. Finally, they should be familiar with and able to apply an array of social work methods. Only with a foundation of trust, teamwork, and collaboration will students be supported to take risks and to build their own sense of personal power and autonomy.

Saleebey's original report can be thought of as a blueprint for experiential learning. His more literary and reflective narrative account of the University of Kansas project, "From the 'Garden' of Poverty: Amazing Blooms" (Saleebey, 1996), describes the humanistic implications for the many people touched by this nontraditional project: students, faculty, and consumers. In his essay, Saleebey confirms what I have argued previously, that significant changes in teaching and practice are more likely the products of certain leaders' passion and commitment than of the reasonable deliberations of committees, curriculum planners, and the like. In many ways the project is one more active expression of Saleebey's articulate commitment to social justice first expressed some years ago in an article on the education of radical social workers (Saleebey & Hunter, 1977). He reiterates this commitment in his current essay and advises social work educators that they must visibly demonstrate their own commitment to the pursuit of social justice: "we cannot just climb hortatory scaffolding in the classroom. We must build the lattice-work of our commitments in the world around us" (p. 34).

The public housing community, the "garden of poverty" that was the field setting, now becomes "the world around us," a world at risk because the surrounding community wanted to raze it. A student and faculty member of the University of Kansas School of Social Welfare already were involved in a coalition of residents and members of legal aid and the housing authority created to block this plan. The rhetorical principles that shaped the program's plan in the original report become more earthy in tone when they are translated into the demands of real life. For example, the resolution not to do anything that was not in the interest of residents or leaders turned out to be naïve; the judgments of leaders did not always correspond with the views of their constituencies. The intent to support the strengths and resilience of the residents proved to be a motive that was hard to sustain. So many of the residents were living under siege conditions that there was little time or space for students to think about how to focus on the residents' strengths. Perhaps most important was the discovery that even the best plans and principles could not be devised from the outside looking in. Although being on site revealed much of what otherwise could not be understood and appreciated, one was not really an "insider," a truth to be acknowledged and respected. The essential difference was that students and faculty went home at the end of the day; residents were stuck in their perilous quarters.

There were many "lessons from the garden," as Saleebey put it, that crystallized the values of such on-site experiential learning opportunities. What occurs in the field, "the dailiness of trouble for people struggling in poverty," cannot truly be replicated in the discourse of the classroom. In the field one learns not *about* clients' lives, but *how it is to be* a person caught in such menacing circumstances. To the extent that learners are to be immersed in this "dailiness," they cannot escape knowing with every sense the traumas, crises, and weaknesses as well as the strengths, virtues, and inner resources that evolve out of their struggles with adversity. Classrooms and textbooks by their very nature present human experience in disjointed ways. In the empirical world of field practice, experience is coherent, whole, integral.

Like the Newcastle project, the University of Kansas nontraditional field placement offers an intimation of an answer to a question posed earlier in this book. I wondered what the profession would look like now if Jane Addams's voice of the settlements had been heeded over the academic soundings of university educators. If her humanistic persuasions about the democratic and moral mission of social work had assumed influence over the "scientific methods serious social work demanded," would the profession be facing its current struggle, not only with its identity but also with the public's impression of it? The report and essay on the Kansas project faintly echo Addams's essay, *A Function of the Social Settlement* (1997/1899). There she spoke of people who had consciously formed themselves into groups to seek spots where the dearth of applied knowledge was most obvious, "the depressed quarters of great cities." Their intent was not to find clinical material but "to use synthetically and directly whatever knowledge they, as a group, may possess, to test its validity and to discover the conditions under which this knowledge may be employed." They were further interested "to test the *value of human knowledge by action and realization*."

We have considered by theory and example how experiential learning can be an effective means for people to learn to become social workers who join with consumers or clients within the entirety of their life circumstances. But the last few paragraphs suggest that this approach to learning is something more than an independent or novel technique, method, or skill. One might say that such learning is also an essential property of social work, part of the profession's heritage. One might also say that it completes a circle. For experiential learning returns us to the roots of social work in Addams's terms. The University of Kansas students in the housing development, or the Newcastle students attempting to make a difference in the field of criminal justice, were, in important ways, meeting the standards and principles of good social work.

If there is a point on the arc where the circle can begin, it is at the intersection of the Jane Addams's and John Dewey's thinking. There, amid other incipient movements in social work, we find our beginnings. Although many biographies have been written about these remarkable figures as individuals, less attention has been given to this very unusual story of a relationship of two great minds, each one's genius enriching and nourishing the other's. Addams's conceptions of helping and serving the dispossessed embraced Dewey's ideas of learning and growth; likewise, Dewey's watershed theories of education were grounded (in the earthiest sense of the term) in the real-life turbulence of the settlement movement.

This is what I mean by coming full circle, for in the examples of experiential learning I have described, particularly the nontraditional program of the University of Kansas, we find a sophisticated enactment of the way principles of service and principles of learning inform one another. They blend into something that can be called *praxis,* the occasion where the boundaries separating knowing and doing, theory and practice, thought and action blur and fall away. It is an experience in our work with people when, in ways that defy logical understanding, wisdom, memory, experience, personal talent, and artistry are welded into a sense confident action.

The mission of social work education according to the CSWE (1992) Curriculum Policy Statement is "alleviate poverty, oppression, and discrimination" and to "further the well-being of people and promote social and economic justice." This mission cannot be achieved without the proper educational scheme. The proper educational scheme is also necessary to fulfill Specht and Courtney's (1994) prescription that "social work's mission should be to build a meaning, a purpose, and a sense of obligation for the community. It is only by creating a community that we establish a basis for commitment, obligation and social support" (p. 27).

The goals of the CPS, or Specht and Courtney's (1994) ambitious system of care, both created by vision and hope, are indeed desirable. Surely, we need these visions and hopes as a compass for our pursuit of professional identity and purpose. But as the Kansas program tells us, it is doubtful that these noble ambitions will be realized unless they are supported by an educational philosophy and program that produces professional social workers who have the necessary knowledge and expertise. I believe I have shown that the principles and methods of experiential learning can shape this philosophy and program.

Conclusion

Having said that. . .

The terse phrase, "Having said that,. . ." is such a wonderful rhetorical device. Sandwiched between position statements, the phrase arouses misgivings about what had been, up until that point, a well-crafted, persuasive argument. The reader is left to wonder, "After leading me this far, what's the author up to now?" The author usually follows "Having said that. . ." with some second thoughts on the first argument, a proviso that perhaps tempers or remolds what had seemed sure and credible. The second thoughts that I want to consider are not concerned with the validity of my proposition on experiential learning and social work education. Rather, they are concerned with the kind of reactions that may be aroused by the proposition, reactions that may impede not only a fair and careful reading, but the possibility of the proposition's implementation in the precincts of social work education.

To start with, we know that a considerable gap divides theory from its application in practice. Even the most worthwhile new theory is abrasive to the extent that it may require unfamiliar ways of looking at or dealing with some aspect of the world. New understandings may expand our knowledge, but at the same time they place us in the uncomfortable position of having to reconsider what we were formerly sure was true. An ancient theologian said, "Change is not made without inconvenience, even from worse to better of doing." The inconveniences of change are not received lightly by most institutions. This is frequently the case among such conservative social institutions as colleges, universities, and their professional programs. Faculty meetings, as some know, are sometimes littered with the remnants of well-conceived (but rarely, earth-shaking) proposals for curriculum revisions.

Reflect for a moment on a very obvious but overlooked phenomenon. The books and journals of the profession are chock full of demonstration program findings, empirical studies of effective practice, brilliant reformulations of theory, and new theoretical insights that, logically, functionally, and axiomatically, appear relevant to education and practice. However, at best and over time the translations of these ideas into practice occurs in scattered and limited ways. Researchers are especially vocal about and puzzled by why their persuasive findings meet few buyers in practice or planning.

For this reason it is vital that I take the step that should follow any innovative proposal—that is, to spell out, explore, and advise the reader about some of the objections that might be expected to arise in response to any seemingly radical proposal. The history of ideas (and the paradigmatic predications of Thomas Kuhn) tell us quite clearly that it would be foolish to assume that the merit of an idea alone will assure its acceptance and affirmation. To put it another way, we have all been witness to well-thought out ideas that have failed in practice because someone failed to anticipate the conditions that might disrupt their implementation. Specifically, I want to address the possible sources of resistance to a curricular shift from a teaching model to a humanistic learning model or, putting it another way, from the articulated or traditional model to the experiential learning model of social work education.

Schools of social work have as their mission the promotion of change. But change, more often than not, is for "them," not "us." Change is, for some identified social or personal problems, injustices, and other like conditions, "out there." My earlier analogy of the social work "tree of knowledge" with its deep-set roots and sturdy trunk was not accidental. It symbolizes the durable and unyielding heritage of the evolving traditions and ideologies of social work education. We can also think of this tree as a variation on Kuhn's (1962) concept of a "paradigm." According to Kuhn a paradigm is a set of beliefs that attracts a devoted group of adherents. The set of beliefs, however, is sufficiently open-ended to leave the adherents with all sorts of problems to be solved but only within the boundaries of the paradigm. Such problem solving prepares novices for membership and practice in the particular system.

Ronald Dear (1999) succinctly addresses the pain and inconvenience of change in his advocacy for something as temporal as extending the length of MSW programs, a plan considerably less radical than the changes recommended here. He observes that such a transformation "would encounter immense opposition from those most committed to the current way of doing things. Even discussion of the question is likely to cause directors, deans. . . and faculty substantial discomfort." And, he adds, revision would be "quite contentious as faculty interest groups invariably struggle for their share of academic turf" (p. 395). To be sure, Dear is generalizing about this unhappy state of affairs; perchance there are programs that are both rational and collegial and are able work out curricular changes with a modicum of strife. Still one must anticipate the natural human and organizational reactions that are aroused when change is confronted, when familiar ways of doing things are up for question.

Whether we are talking about a person or a complex of interacting people, resistance to perceived change can appear in two mutually reinforcing forms. The first form is explicit. The experience of implementing the Bristol model described earlier is a good example of explicit reactions to curricular change. Fortunately, the initial resistance was resolved though some political good luck. Ronald Dear (1999) also discusses explicit obstacles likely to impede the implementation of his plan to extend the length of the MSW program. According to Dear, such a transformation

> would take time, be difficult and expensive to implement.... It would require complicated and difficult reconceptualization, reconfiguration, and likely revision of the MSW curriculum, and likely revision of BSW and doctoral programs. . . . As anyone experienced in curriculum change could attest, even minor revisions tend to encounter tremendous resistance from both administration and faculty. (pp. 395–396)

The second form of resistance to perceived change is of a more diffuse and implicit nature. It expresses the ingrained culture of the institution—its assumptions, values, and norms, as well as the narrative it has created about itself, its history, its ideologies, and its mission. These elements encompass an undisputed way of thinking and acting that in everyday academic life often boils down to "That's how we've always done things around here."

To be more specific about this implicit level of resistance to change in professional social work education, let me comment on some special constituents of the culture of the institution. They include the role and status of the social work academic, the ambiguous stance of the social work field instructor, employer demands on social workers, and the authority of the textbook industry. These constitutents are forces to be reckoned with in any proposal for curricular change. They are important not only because they define and influence the nature of social work education, but also because they reinforce the equilibrium and continuity of the educational institution, its curricular structure, and especially the long-standing division between class and practicum.

I place the social work academic at the head of the list because this figure, symbolically, is at the fulcrum of change, or more functionally, serves as the gatekeeper for change. To be employed as a teacher at the highest levels of education (in contrast with the requirements for teaching at primary or secondary levels) requires only that the candidate has earned an advanced degree in an appropriate field of study. In their recent study, "Preparing Practitioners for the Professoriate," Dinerman, Feldman, and Ello (1999) surveyed all doctoral programs in social work in the United States and found an absence of required courses designed to prepare students for teaching and the faculty role. If the candidate is demonstrably knowledgeable, an expert in a specific content area, it is not considered necessary that he or she be equipped with a foundation of educational theory, principles, and methods of teaching. There is no apparent need for the training required to assure that one's expert knowledge will be transmitted in effective ways. It is safe to say that those who become good teachers over time likely achieve this role through ad hoc experiential learning, trial and error, collegial interaction, and learning from students.

Academic freedom is a major and cherished attribute of the professor's role. The freedom to teach a course as one pleases avoids entropy, helps maintain the steady state of the institution, and strengthens the educator's identity with the larger institution. Within some very broad boundaries and depending on one's responsibilities within the curriculum, the educator has the liberty to teach and pursue knowledge and discuss it openly without restriction or interference. This means that even within a special content area of social work education (in contrast to education in the physical sciences) there is bound to be considerable variation in how that content is taught, variation that expresses the personal attributes and world views of the individual teachers. Similar disparities exist in other divisions of the curriculum. Although these examples of academic freedom allow for invention, flexibility, and experimentation, we must keep in mind that they are implemented within the more or less impermeable structure of American higher education more specifically, the CSWE Curriculum Policy Statement.

My intent is not to critique, but merely to sketch the culture of social work education to show how it might bear on resistance to the proposal to consider the experiential education model. Perhaps "resistance" has too many pejorative implications. Perhaps it is more prudent to say that modern educators are more invested in *maintaining and improving* the existing model of education than they are in embracing a new one. This intent is clearly evident in the profusion of scholarly books and articles (many cited in these pages) that are aimed at refining and strengthening this model. Given the educational background of social work academics, that they themselves are products the model of education they use, one must ask why would other options appear desirable or feasible? Perhaps the answer lies in Minnich's (1990) critical observation, cited earlier, that academics forget, once they become authorities in their own field, what they endured as lowly graduate students. Once certified, many proceed to defend their own views of what "properly" constitutes their discipline with the same totalizing vehemence from which they once suffered (p. 172).

However this antipathy to change might be explained or rationalized, the exceptional role and status of the social work academic within the profession also poses a set of problems relative to the imbalance between class and field faculty. Mesbur and Glassman (1991) alluded to this problem in their outline of the dilemmas that face social work field education. The unequal status of class and field faculty blocks achievement of the rational principles of integration, faculty commitment, and mutuality that are required to assure the integrity and effectiveness of the field instruction component of the curriculum. How is it possible to achieve a working spirit of integration, faculty commitment, and mutuality when striking disparities exist between the classroom and field faculties? The power, privilege, and credentialed status of the academic faculty are scarcely enjoyed by field faculty. Typically, field faculty have little to say about selection of students for admission, and at best they might play an ancillary role in the design and development of the academic program (most likely they are on the receiving end of these decisions). Field based instructors are generally not part of the continuing discussion and deliberation on the program among university based faculty in both formal and casual ways. And field instructors, required to balance the standards imposed by the educational program against the demands of their employing agency, are often torn by conflicting responsibilities.

It is worth recalling the consequences of this predicament noted in a study of the teaching methods of field instructors (Rogers & McDonald, 1995). The instructors in the study did not subscribe to any formal approach to field education, but instead used only what was expedient in producing students who were ready to learn how to be professional practitioners. Because of role strain and time constraints, they relied on methods that were most effective and least time consuming from their point of view. Based on this sample, we can assume that, in their various settings, other field instructors create different pathways to learning, relying on intuitive forms of experiential learning in preparing their students for practice. They are equal to using an on-the-spot learning model of education because of their active and intimate involvement with their students within the demanding pragmatics of practice. Still, although these approaches might prove to be very effective, they do not realize the desired ideal of integration, commitment, and mutuality that would resolve the disjuncture of class and field.

Clearly, field teachers have much to offer the profession about the real-life, experiential nature of learning. They are not dealing with the abstract, the virtual, and the theoretical; they know first hand the humanistic anomalies that are peculiar to learning, growth, and change that are not inscribed in textbooks or curricular objectives. They cope with both the ardent learner and the stumbler; they know what works and what doesn't. Lacking the status of their academic counterparts, field instructors, with some exceptions and for many good reasons, do not publish or otherwise articulate their perspectives on learning; therefore, their influence on curricular change of any kind cannot be particularly compelling.

Another form of resistance to curricular change is expressed in the needs and dictates of agencies and the practice community in general. It is not necessary to spend much time on this issue since educational programs perennially face challenges posed by local social services. Schools of social work struggle to keep in step with the ever-changing conditions and problems of their communities. But the conservative nature of academic scholarship and the inability to predict the emergence or morbidity of the next set of "troubles" leaves them vulnerable to the appeals of agencies to equip graduates with the special practice knowledge and skills required to meet this or that immediate demand of service. Currently, even overriding these specialized demands, the sweeping tide of managed care has, according to Brooks and Riley (1996), "created dramatic changes in social work agencies and in student training." In this study of the effects of managed health care, the authors surveyed field instructors and graduate students to discover its impact on current practice demands. Their findings confirmed impressions of agency stress and the increased need for new and brief forms of treatment. The demands of managed care have exacerbated exacerbating pressures on the academic program to conform to the needs of the practice community.

In rounding out this discussion of forces impinging on the integrity of the standard curriculum, let us not forget that the lure of private practice and the field of clinical social work also pose demands for augmenting theories and methods of treatment in curriculum content. In sum, although these many demands are not in themselves obstacles to serious curricular change, the sense of urgency that is evoked tends to divert the energies of all concerned to searching for solutions to the immediate predicament. Thus the time and thought required for considering novel and alternative approaches to teaching and learning becomes a remote luxury.

Finally, the commercial textbook industry also tends, albeit in more oblique ways, to regulate and support the steady state of the standard curriculum and the commanding status of the classroom. One needs only to stroll the aisles of exhibitors at the CSWE Annual Program Meeting and visit the many booths of publishers to detect their influence on social work education. Their primary aim is to sell textbooks, to persuade faculty to adopt their products for classroom use. Competition among these purveyors is not based on quality or innovation, but on the cosmetic attractiveness of their books, the teaching aids and exercises that are included, content that will not tax the reader's energy, and other alluring features. One should be astonished by the supermarket effect of the displays. One can shop for a compendium on theories and methods, still another book on generalist practice, or narrow and highly specialized works on most any condition, generation, population, gender issue, or personal and social ailment that a social worker might encounter in practice. And if conference attendees need a little respite, many publishers offer potential patrons such festivities as ice cream socials, wine and cheese events, giveaways, and treats of all kinds.

For the many teachers who rely on textbooks, this industry is an important source of knowledge, a practical font of information for teaching student social workers. Thus, by definition, the textbook industry influences what is taught and learned and, at the same time, reinforces the existing assumption that the classroom is where serious learning is supposed to occur, that it is truly the center of enlightenment. To be sure, one can find the occasional text for field instructors, but these books either support the existing class-field arrangement or strive to redefine the practicum as a distinct sector of learning in itself.

The most crucial point bearing on education for practice is that most textbooks, even in their many variations, are conservative in substance, preserving the received wisdom or state of the art of the profession. Commercial publishers are notoriously reluctant to accept manuscripts that are not mainstream, that suggest alternative and fresh theories and models, that are reflective and critical, or that do not complement the objectives of specific courses. What will sell in large numbers is what matters, and, of course, what will sell is the familiar. What remain as resources for the critical or innovative author are university presses (that for many reasons, often economic, are becoming increasingly mainstream) and, gratefully, the presses of professional organizations like NASW and CSWE.

One more form of resistance to change, one of a different order, needs to be added to this list. This has to do with the question of how the experiential learning model would be implemented in modern social work education. There are no straightforward answers to this question. Implementing an entirely new learning model is not like simply incorporating a special model, a framework of knowledge and practice, or a unit of study. In short, this model is not a commodity or asset that can simply be patched on to an existing curriculum. The experiential learning model is not about content. Rather, it represents a philosophy and theory of how people learn that not only supplants the current traditional or articulated model of social work education, but also redefines the relationship between field and class. Thus, the plan to implement an experiential approach in one way or another must engage everyone in the careful study of the principles and assumptions that support this approach and a commitment to them. The endeavor to set this plan in motion will determine the route that will be taken. In other words, the intent to reach a certain destination requires charting a course that will take into account not only to the constraints just described, but also the political climate of the educational environment, the realistic limits of the effort, and how it will be evaluated. Let me recall examples of the adoption or application of the principles of experiential learning previously discussed to make this point more graphically.

In the case of the University of Newcastle, the social work program's embrace of the experiential learning model conformed with the university's overall commitment to what it called a "problem-based" approach to education. In other words, the university itself established its own educational foundations of learning as a guide and rationale for every department or discipline including, of course, the department of social work. Within the educational matrix created by the university, the social work department developed its "ownership" of the problem-based approach by relying on the benefits of group processes involving all faculty and students. Using the problem-based approach itself, they collectively worked out a curriculum plan that expressed the department's convictions on what constitutes excellence in social work education as integral to lifetime learning.

The Bristol social work program, in contrast, had to contend with a more challenging task when it attempted to establish its ELA model within the traditionally normative regulations of the greater university. Although political good fortune overcame the regulatory hurdles of university administration, the success of the program, as was the case at Newcastle, derived from the intensive front-end planning and deliberation involving staff and students. In a collegial climate created and guided by faculty who were committed to the experiential design, everyone was expected to participate in preliminary explorations of the educational philosophy supporting experiential learning, taking account of its costs, benefits, and anticipated outcomes.

The two American adventures with experiential learning, certainly more modest and experimental, than the preceding examples, differ from them also in being primarily practicum centered. In both instances, the essential curricular structure of the social work program was not altered; only field settings were used for practical and experimental purposes. The University of Kansas set up a new, nontraditional field program, an interesting blend of complementary ends and means. The end was to provide services to consumers who are typically underserved by traditional helping systems; the means was an innovative field placement employing Kolb's and others' principles of experiential learning. The belief was that the learner-centeredness of the experiential model would enable students to discover their personal forms and styles of learning that would result in more creative and responsive ways of helping their marginalized clients.

The study of Raschick and colleagues (1998) was more experimental in design. Applying Kolb's learning style model to one of the typical field education settings of a social work program, the intent was to determine whether the use of this model would improve the quality of students' satisfaction with their field education, their student-field supervisor relationships, and, of course, their learning styles and work with clients.

One cannot put the proverbial cart before the horse. Taking into account the many caveats just described, the implementation of this educational model must follow a positive evaluation of its merits and potentialities for achieving excellence in the education and performance of people who desire to learn how to become social workers.

Summing Up

How does one learn to become a social worker? This question opened this book. It launched an inquiry into the ideas, perspectives and debates that have resulted in the current state of social work education, and an inquiry into current and developing theories of learning. The best answer to the question of how people learn to become social workers is that they do it through the process of experiential learning. This conclusion suggests that there needs to be some serious reconsideration of the traditional teaching model of social work education that divides the educational scheme into two often discontinuous arenas: the university based classroom considered the primary site of learning, where students acquire the necessary knowledge, and the practicum, where it is assumed that this knowledge can be applied to demands of practice learning. In the alternative learning model I have argued for in these pages, the learner-centered field or practicum would be at the heart of social work education, with the classroom serving to support or complement field learning by providing the knowledge students require to achieve their learning objectives as emerging professionals.

The complex answers to this question are by no means restricted to the education of social workers. Learning is an active process that occurs in the real world of everyday experience as well as in pursuits of knowledge, competency, and growth within any particular field. As Donald Schön's (1983) pathbreaking work on reflection-in-action shows, reflection is a process that is at the core of the practice of many professionals—whether they are scientists, psychotherapists, or managers—who are not locked into a view of themselves as mere technical experts. Experiential learning, in which reflection plays a key role, is a humanistic and democratic alternative to traditional forms of education that emphasize expertise and skill, what Schön calls *technical rationality*—technical problem solving based on specialized scientific knowledge. Experiential learning also involves a shift from the traditional teaching model where the teacher as the expert determines what needs to be taught and learned, to a learning model that is student centered, based on assumptions about how people learn, and which occurs within a climate of collegiality and discourse. Within such a climate, learning that is both practical and creative is possible.

The learner-based experiential model of education now gaining increasing currency, was articulated with exceptional clarity and depth 75 years ago in John Dewey's writing. Like current learning theorists, Dewey was concerned with interaction, reflection, and experience within a democratic and community context. He believed that learning involved an engagement with and a reconstruction of experience. His convictions have influenced and inspired leading educational scholars like Kolb, Gardner, Menand, Rorty, and Schön. Dewey could not have foreseen that his philosophic speculations and self-created theories about experience would eventually be confirmed by sciences that did not exist in his time—developmental psychology, cognitive science, and neuroscience.

Recent findings in the research on the plasticity of the brain have given us a more complete picture of how intellectual development occurs. One of the key principles of behavioral neuroscience is that experience can modify brain structure *long after brain development is complete* (Kolb, & Whishaw, 1998). Thus, as

Bransford, Brown, and Cocking (1999) report, learning, as an experience, changes the physical structure of the brain. In turn, these structural changes alter the functional organization of the brain or, to put in another way, learning as experience organizes and reorganizes the brain. This finding closely corresponds with Dewey's position that experience is a means of reconstructing reality since it can be assumed that the reorganization of the brain will result in changes in perception of reality as the learner interacts with his or her environment. This brief reference offers yet another salient reason for all institutions dedicated to learning and change to be cognizant of this of new knowledge. As excited as we become about the new technologies that are transforming traditional conventions governing *how to teach*, the results of the research of the neurosciences should be transforming our understanding about the role of experience in *how people learn and change.*

I search for satisfactory ways to bring this monograph to a close, to, in effect, end the journey. But none makes itself known. Perhaps the reason is that all that yet needs to be said about how one learns to become a social worker still cannot be finally said. Learning, as I have tried to show is ongoing, open-ended, subject to unsuspected contingencies, always in process—and, ideally, lifelong. One would not know this, judging by the efforts to enclose curricula and programmatic structures within rigid and accreditational bounds or to reduce what needs to be learned only to "proven" empirical methods and techniques. Learning to be a member of our profession (or for that matter, any helping profession) will, by definition, continue to be unconfined, responsive to real-life circumstances, and, one hopes, reflective and imaginative.

In some meaningful ways, even for the most seasoned practitioner, the first encounter with a client or community is a new learning (or relearning) event that places one's perception of reality at risk. And there are the larger scale emergencies—economic hardships, sudden catastrophes, surges of depression and oppression, and other unexampled calamities—that invade our intentions to be of help. They compel the reflective practitioner to relearn how to cope with the new experience and, of greater consequence, to grow from the struggle to overcome such adversities.

Thus, in professional life as in real-life, there are no conclusions or closings. At the most there is perhaps a moment for a pause or deep breath. Cases don't close, even as case records are relegated to the file cabinet. Clients go on with their lives, doing what they can with their inexorable adventures of living. The plans we devise are never fully consummated; their effects become part of the evolution of ideas and actions that follow. Few conclusive results are generated by research; we are gratified if we discover better questions or new directions for inquiry.

The realization that learning in its broadest sense is interminable may, at some moments, endow us with a vague sense of immortality. With so very much to know and understand, with all there is to discover about ourselves, others, and our world of experience, it is hard to conceive of an ending, a time when each of us can say with complete certainty, "Now I know."

References

Aase, G. (1982). A history of social work field instruction. In B. W. Sheafor & L. E. Jenkins (Eds.), *Quality field instruction in social work* (pp.37-60). New York: Longman.

Abbott, E. (1931). *Social welfare and professional education*. Chicago: University of Chicago Press.

Addams, J. (1997). *A function of the social settlement* (pp. 273-286). In L. Menand (Ed.), *Pragmatism: A Reader*. New York: Vintage Books. (Originally published 1899)

Bawden, R. (1987). Problem based learning: An Australian perspective. In D. Boud (Ed.), *Problem based learning in education for the professions*. Sydney, Australia: Higher Education Research and Development Society of Australia.

Berlin, I. (1990). *The crooked timber of humanity*. Princeton, NJ: Princeton University Press.

Bogo, M., & Vayda, E. (1998). *The practice of field instruction in social work: Theory and process*. New York: Columbia University Press.

Bransford, J. D., Brown, A. L., & Cocking, R. R. (Eds.). (1999). *How people learn: Brain, mind, experience, and school*. Washington, DC: National Academy Press.

Brooks, D., & Riley, P. (1996). The impact of managed health care policy on student field training. *Smith College Studies in Social Work*, *66*(3), 307-316.

Bruner, J. (1996). *The culture of education*. Cambridge, MA: Harvard University Press.

Burgess, H. (1992). *Problem-led learning for social work: The Enquiry and Action Approach*. London: Whiting and Birch.

Burgess, H., & Jackson, S. (1990). Enquiry and action learning: A new approach to social work education. *Social Work Education*, *9*(3) 3-19.

Camp, G. (1999). Problem-based learning: A paradigm shift or a passing fad? *Medical Education Hotline, University of Texas Medical Branch.*

Cott, N. (1987). *The grounding of modern feminism.* New Haven, CT: Yale University Press.

Council on Social Work Education. (1992). *Curriculum policy statement for baccalaureate and master's degree programs in social work education.* Alexandria, VA: Author.

Curriculum Handbook. (1997–1998). Cleveland, OH: Case Western University School of Medicine.

Davis, L. (1985). Female and male voices in social work. *Social Work, 30,* 106-113.

Dean, R. G. (1995). Stories of AIDS: The use of narrative as an approach to understanding in an AIDS support group. *Clinical Social Work Journal, 23*(3), 287-304.

Dear, R. B. (1999). Should MSW curricula be extended to three years? Yes! *Journal of Social Work Education, 35,* 395-398.

De Bono, E. (1973). *Lateral thinking: Creativity step by step.* New York: Harper and Row.

Dewey, J. (1916). *Democracy and education: An introduction to the philosophy of education.* New York: Macmillan.

Dewey, J. (1925). *Experience and nature.* Chicago: Open Court.

Dewey, J. (1938). *Experience and education.* New York: Macmillan.

Dinerman, M., Feldman, P., & Ello, L. (1999). Preparing practitioners for the professoriate. *Journal of Teaching in Social Work, 18*(1/2), 23-32.

English, B., Gaha, J., & Gibbons, J. (1994). Preparing social workers for an uncertain future. In S. Chen, R. Cowdroy, A. Kingsland, & M. Ostwald (Eds.), *Reflections on problem based learning* (pp. 279-296). Sydney, Australia: Australian Problem Based Learning Network.

Flexner, A. (2000). *Is social work a profession?* In L. Leighninger, *Creating a new profession: The beginnings of social work education in the United States* (pp. 39-47). Alexandria, VA: Council on Social Work Education. (Originally published 1915)

Florida International University Digital Library [Online]. (1999). Available at http://fiudl.diu.edu.

Flynn, L. (1997). Social work students confront social justice issues through experiential learning. *Australian Social Work, 50*(4), 21-27.

Freire, P. (1973a). *Education for critical consciousness.* New York: Seabury.

Freire, P. (1973b). *Education: The practice of freedom.* London: Writers and Readers Publishing Cooperative.

Freire, P. (1973c). *Pedagogy of the oppressed.* New York: Seabury.

Freire, P. (1998). *Pedagogy of freedom: Ethics democracy, and civic courage.* New York: Rowman and Littlefield.

Galper, J. (1980). *Social work practice: A radical perspective.* Englewood Cliffs, NJ: Prentice Hall.

Gardner, H. (1983). *Frames of mind: The theory of multiple intelligences.* New York: Basic Books.

Gardner, H. (1991). *The unschooled mind: How children think and how schools should teach.* New York: Basic Books.

Gardner, H. (1993a). *Creating minds: An anatomy of creativity seen through the lives of Freud, Einstein, Picasso, Stravinsky, Eliot, Graham, and Gandhi.* New York: Basic Books.

Gardner, H. (1993b). *Multiple intelligences: The theory in practice.* New York: Basic Books.

Gibbons, J. (1992). The teaching team: Small group process in social work education. In S. L. Regan (Ed.), *Social group work monograph* (Vol.3). Sydney, Australia: University of New South Wales.

Goldstein, H. (1981a). Generalist social work practice. In H. Specht & N. Gilbert (Eds.), *Handbook of the social services* (pp. 413-433). Englewood Cliffs, NJ: Prentice Hall.

Goldstein, H. (1981b). *Social learning and change: A cognitive approach to human services.* Columbia, SC: University of South Carolina Press.

Graham, P. A. (1998, Winter). Educational dilemmas for Americans. *Daedalus*, pp. 225-235.

Graybeal, C. T., & Ruff, E. (1995). Process recording: It's more than you think. *Journal of Social Work Education, 31*, 169-181.

Hamilton, A., & Else, J. F. (1983). *Designing field education.* Springfield, IL: Charles C. Thomas.

Hartman, A. (1990). Education for direct practice. *Families in Society*, *71*(1), 44-50.

Hollis, E. V., & Taylor, A. L. (1951). *Social work education in the United States*. New York: Columbia University Press.

Higher Education Funding Council for England. (1994). *Quality assessment report by HEFCE for University of Bristol Applied Social Work* [Online]. Available at http://www.niss.ac.uk/education/hefce/qar/q152-94.html.

Kitchener, K. S., & King, P. M. (1981). Reflective judgment: Concepts of and their relationship to age and education. *Journal of Applied Developmental Psychology*, *2*, 89-116.

Knefelkamp, L., & Schneider, C. (1997). Education for a world lived in common with others. In R. Orrill (Ed.), *Education and democracy: Re-imagining liberal learning in America* (pp. 327-345). New York: College Entrance Examination Board.

Knowles, M. B., & Associates (1984). *Andragogy in action: Applying modern principles of adult learning*. San Francisco: Jossey-Bass.

Koestler, A. (1964). *The act of creation*. New York: Dell.

Kolb, B., & Whishaw, I. Q. (1998). Brain plasticity and behavior [Review]. *Annual Review of Psychology*, *49*, 43-64.

Kolb, D. A. (1984). *Experiential learning: Experience as the source of learning and development*. Englewood Cliffs, NJ: Prentice Hall.

Kolenda, K. (1990). *Rorty's humanistic pragmatism*. Tampa: University of South Florida Press.

Kuhn, T. (1962). *The structure of scientific revolutions*. Chicago: University of Chicago Press.

Kunzel, R. (1993). *Fallen women, problem girls: Unmarried mothers and the professionalization of social work, 1890–1945*. New Haven, CT: Yale University Press.

Kupiec, T. Y. (1993). *Rethinking tradition: Integrating service with academic study on college campuses*. Providence, RI: Campus Compact.

Lagemann, E. C. (1997). From discipline-based to problem-centered learning. In R. Orrill (Ed.), *Education and democracy: Re-imagining liberal learning in America* (pp. 21-44). New York: College Entrance Examination Board.

Laird, J. (1989). Women and stories: Restorying women's self-constructions. In M. McGoldrick, C. M. Anderson, & F. Walsh (Eds.), *Women in families: A framework for family therapy* (pp. 427-450). New York: Norton.

Langer, E. J. (1997). *The power of mindful learning.* New York: Addison-Wesley.

Lee, P. (1929) Presidential address. *National Conference on Social Welfare Proceedings, 56*, p. 5.

Lempert, D. H. (1996). *Escape from the ivory tower: Student adventures in democratic experiential education.* San Francisco: Jossey Bass.

Lindemann, E. C. (1949). Science and philosophy: Sources of human faith. In Community Service Society of New York, *Social work as human relations: Anniversary papers of the New York School of Social Work and the Community Service Society of New York.* New York: Columbia University Press.

Lunbeck, E. (1994). *The psychiatric persuasion.* Princeton, NJ: Princeton University Press.

Lundblad, K. S. (1995). Jane Addams and social reform: A role model for the 1990s. *Social Work, 40*, 661-669.

Malekoff, A. (1997). *Group work with adolescents.* New York: Guilford.

Marsiglia, F. (1991). *The ethnic warriors: Ethnic identity and school achievement as perceived by a group of selected mainland Puerto Rican students.* Unpublished doctoral dissertation, Case Western Reserve University, Cleveland, OH.

Menand, L. (1997). Re-imagining liberal education. In R. Orrill (Ed.), *Education and democracy: Re-imagining liberal education in America* (pp. 1-20). New York: College Examination Board.

Mesbur, E. S., & Glassman, U. (1991). From commitment to curriculum: The humanistic foundations of field instruction. In D. Schneck, B. Grossman, & U. Glassman (Eds.), *Field education in social work* (pp. 47-58). Dubuque, IA: Kendall/Hunt.

Minnich, E. M. (1990). *Transforming knowledge.* Philadelphia: Temple University Press.

Montessori, M. (1967). *The absorbent mind.* New York: Holt, Rinehart & Winston.

Moore, D. T. (1990). Experiential education as critical discourse. In

J. C. Kendall & Associates, *Combining service and learning: A resource book for community and public service* (pp. 273-281). Raleigh, NC: National Society for Internships and Experiential Education.

Myers, L. M., & Thyer, B. A. (1997). Should social work clients have the right to effective treatment? *Social Work, 42*, 228-298.

National Association of Social Workers. (1996). *Code of ethics*. Washington, DC: Author.

Ostrow, J., Hesser, G., & Enos, S., (Eds.). (1999). *Cultivating the sociological imagination: Concepts and models for service-learning in sociology*. Washington, DC: American Association for Higher Education.

Pelech, W., Stalker, C. A., Regehr, C., & Jacobs, M. (1999). Making the grade: The quest for validity in admissions decisions. *Journal of Social Work Education, 35*, 215-226.

Rainey, M. A., & Kolb, D. A. (1995). Using experiential learning theory and learning styles in diversity education. In R. R. Sims, & S. J. Sims (Eds.), *The importance of learning styles* (pp. 129-146). Westport, CT: Greenwood.

Raschick, M., Maypole, D. E., & Day, P. (1998). Improving field education through Kolb learning theory. *Journal of Social Work Education, 34*, 31- 42.

Reynolds, B. (1942). *Learning and teaching in the practice of social work*. New York: Farrar & Rinehart.

Richmond, M. (1917). *Social diagnosis*. New York: Russell Sage Foundation.

Robinson, V. (1930). *A changing psychology in social casework*. Chapel Hill: University of North Carolina Press.

Rogers, G. (1996). Training field instructors British style. *Journal of Social Work Education, 32*, 365-276.

Rogers, G., & McDonald, P. L. (1995). Expedience over education: Teaching methods used by field instructors. *The Clinical Supervisor, 13*(2), 41-65.

Rorty, R. (1989). *Contingency, irony, and solidarity*. Cambridge, MA: Cambridge University Press.

Saleebey, D. (1996, Summer). From the "garden" of poverty: Amazing blooms. *Reflections: Narratives of Professional Helping, 2*(3), 34-45.

Saleebey, D. (1997). *Report on nontraditional field placements*. Unpublished manuscript, School of Social Work, University of Kansas.

Saleebey, D. (1998). *Theory and the generation and subversion of knowledge*. Unpublished manuscript, School of Social Work, University of Kansas.

Saleebey, D. (1999). Building a knowledge base: A personal account. *Families in Society, 80*(6), 652-661.

Saleebey, D., & Hunter, M. (1977). Spirit and substance: Beginnings in the education of radical social workers. *Journal of Social Work Education, 13*, 60-67.

Schneck, D. (1991). Ideal and reality. In D. Schneck, B. Grossman, & U. Glassman (Eds.), *Field education in social work* (pp. 17-35). Dubuque, IA: Kendall/Hunt.

Schön, D. (1983). *The reflective practitioner*. New York: Basic Books.

Schön, D. (1987). *Educating the reflective practitioner*. San Francisco: Jossey-Bass.

Sheafor, B. W., & Jenkins, L. E. (Eds.). (1982). An overview of social work field instruction. In B. W. Sheafor & L. E. Jenkins (Eds.), *Quality field instruction in social work*. New York: Longman.

Sims, S. J., & Sims, R. R. (Eds.). (1995). *The importance of learning styles*. Westport, CT: Greenwood.

Sklar, K. K. (1985). The Hull House in the 1890s: A community of women reformers. *Signs, 10*(4), 658-677.

Specht, H., & Courtney, M. (1994). *Unfaithful angels: How social work has abandoned its mission*. New York: Free Press.

Starr, P. (1982). *The social transformation of American medicine*. New York: Basic Books.

Stroup, H. (1960). Social work's new era. In National Conference on Social Welfare, *Social welfare forum, 1960* (pp. 67-78). New York: Columbia University Press.

Taft, J. (1935). *The dynamics of therapy in a controlled relationship*. New York: Macmillan.

Tasker, M. (1999). You like Tupac, Mary? *Families in Society, 80*(3), 216-218.

Taylor, B., & Taylor, A. (1993). Wayfinding training for the severely mentally ill. *Families in Society, 74*, 434-440.

Taylor, B., & Taylor, A. (1997). Social work with ambulatory clients: The wayfinding domain. *Families in Society*, *78*, 299-306.

Thyer, B. A., & Myers, L. I. (1998). Supporting the client's right to effective treatment. *Social Work*, *43*(1), 87-91.

Towle, C. (1954). *The learner in education for the professions as seen in the education for social work*. Chicago: University of Chicago Press.

Watzlawick, P. (1978). *The language of change*. New York: Basic Books.

Weil, S. W., & McGill, I. (Eds.). (1989). A framework for making sense of experiential learning. In S. W. Weil & I. McGill (Eds.), *Making sense of experiential learning: Diversity in theory and practice* (pp. 3-24). Philadelphia: The Society for Research into Higher Education and Open University Press.

Weiner, J. (1999). *Time, love, and memory: A great biologist and his quest for the origins of behavior*. New York: Knopf.

Weiskopf, V. (1979, Autumn). Art and science. *American Scholar*, pp. 473-486.

Westin, D. (1998, September 7). Eulogy. *Time*, pp. 29.

White, M., & Epston, D. (1990). *Narrative means to therapeutic ends*. New York: Norton.

Index

F

G

H